Name ____________________________________

Put stars in the sky. Make the first letter of your name.

Family Time

Chapter 1: God Made Me

In this lesson the children learned that God made them and that they are precious in God's sight. They heard that they are special and can do wonderful things. Your child made a star-shaped name tag because we are like stars shining for God when we try to do our best.

Your Child

Children's self-concepts are formed primarily in the home. Ask your child to tell how he or she is special and to demonstrate one of his or her own gifts. Praise your child frequently.

Reflect

I have called you by name: you are mine. You are precious in my eyes, and I love you.
(adapted from Isaiah 43:1,4)

Pray

God, help us always remember that we are your precious children.

Do

- Tell your child why he or she is special to you.
- Think of a particular talent your child has and then plan how to develop it.
- Take your child outside to look at the stars. You may have to go to an unlighted spot in order to see them well.
- Pray with your child, thanking God for your child's special gifts as well as for his or her eyes, ears, nose, arms, and legs.
- Read to your child *Me I Am!* by Jack Prelutsky. Help your child identify traits and gifts that make him or her special and unique. Praise God for making each of us special.

For more family resources, refer to the Family Activity Booklet and visit **www.loyolapress.com/preschool.**

Name ________________________________

Draw flowers in Jesus' hand.

Family Time

Chapter 2: God Made My Family

In this lesson the children learned that God gave them families. Families are people who live together and love one another. Families vary—some are large, some small; some have just one parent; some include grandparents. Family members try to help one another. Your child made a picture as a gift for your family. Display it in a prominent place. Ask your child to tell who the people are in the picture on this page.

Your Child

Children need to know about their family background. Tell your child stories about yourself and other relatives, including grandparents, aunts, and uncles.

Reflect

Jesus went with Mary and Joseph to Nazareth and was obedient to them. Jesus grew in wisdom and age and favor before all.
(adapted from Luke 2:51–52)

Pray

Loving God, help our family grow in love and holiness.

Do

- Talk with your child about the ways each member of your family helps the others. Point out how your child contributes to the family.
- Visit or call family members.
- Go through a family album with your child or, if you don't have one, start one.
- Plan a family night once a week.
- Develop in your child the habit of praying for family members each night before going to bed.
- Read to your child *All Kinds of Families* by Norma Simon. Talk about the people who are part of your family. Together ask God to bless each person in your family.

For more family resources, refer to the Family Activity Booklet and visit **www.loyolapress.com/preschool.**

So a mitten for her kitten Mother sat and knit.
When Kitty tried it on she found it was a PURRfect fit.
"Oh, thank you, Mom," she said at once, giving her a hug.

Then ready for a catnap, Kitty curled up on the rug.

A Kitten's Tale

Kitty Cat and brother Tom came home one day from school.
Mr. Cat was cooking. Mom was working with a tool.
"Oh, no!" meowed poor Kitty Cat. "It seems I've lost a mitten."
Her whiskers twitched. Her eyes filled up. She cried. Poor, little kitten.

Name ____________________

"Don't cry, my dear," said Kitty's mom. "It's no catastrophe."

Tom purred, "Don't worry. I'll go back and see where it can be."

Mom gave Kitty catnip, and Dad made her some tea.

He said, "We'll find your mitten. Just you wait and see."

2

Through some catalogs they looked. One mitten no one sold.

They looked all through the rag bag and found one that was too old.

Tom came back with empty paws; no mitten could he find.

"I'll knit a mitten," Mother said, "and make it the same kind."

3

By

Name ______________________________

Draw a line from the person who needs help to a friend who is helping.

Family Time

Chapter 3: God Made My Friends

In this lesson the children learned that friends are a gift from God. They talked about their friends. They saw that Jesus had friends and wants to be their friend too. The children came to realize that friends help one another. Your child made a flower. Ask him or her to tell you about it.

Your Child

It is important that children interact with other children at this age in order to develop social skills. Encourage your child to play with others.

Reflect

Jesus said, "You are my friends."
(adapted from John 15:14)

Pray

Jesus, help us be good friends to you and others.

Do

- Talk to your child about your friends and about your neighbors. Point out how you help one another.
- Help your child do something nice for a friend: pick out a birthday present, bake cookies, invite the friend to accompany your family on a trip.
- Plan a party and invite your child's friends.
- Take your child and his or her friends out for lunch or on a picnic.
- Talk to your child about Jesus and read children's books about him to your child.
- Read to your child *Frog and Toad Together* by Arnold Lobel. Talk about what makes a person a good friend. Thank God for the gift of friends.

For more family resources, refer to the Family Activity Booklet and visit **www.loyolapress.com/preschool.**

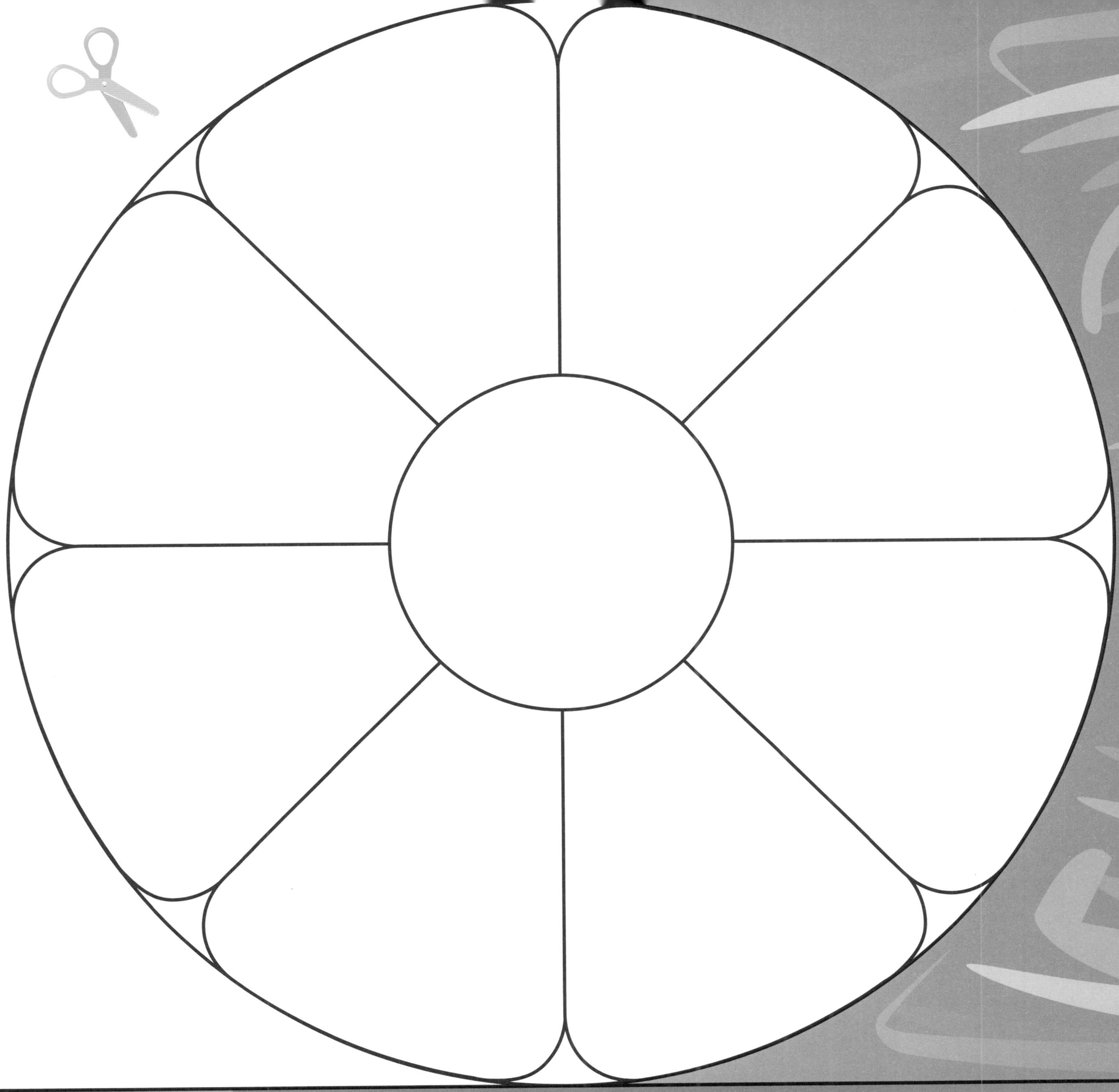

I love you.

name ____________________

Name ________________________________

Circle anyone who has helped you.

Family Time

Chapter 4: God Made My Helpers

In this lesson the children learned about many people who help them. They were guided to obey these helpers. They thought about how their parents assist people through their work. The children heard that Jesus helped many people and that he still helps us today through others. Your child made a card for someone who helps him or her. Let your child tell you about this card. Help him or her deliver it if necessary.

Your Child

Praise your child's efforts to be a helper at home.

Reflect

To each individual the manifestation of the Spirit is given for some benefit.
(1 Corinthians 12:7)

Pray

Holy Spirit, help us use our gifts to help others.

Do

- Take your child to work with you one day.
- Talk about the helpers in your child's life and what they do.
- Make a book of helpers with your child, using magazine and newspaper pictures.
- Try to name with your child all the people who made possible one meal on your table.
- Teach your child to say "please" and "thank you" for others' help.
- Let your child help with tasks, such as making beds, picking up toys, and folding laundry.
- Read to your child a book in the *Curious George* series by Margret and H. A. Rey in which George visits someone in a helping profession. Recall an experience your child has had with a person who helps others. Ask God to show you ways to be a helper to others.

For more family resources, refer to the Family Activity Booklet and visit **www.loyolapress.com/preschool.**

You're the best!

Thank you for helping me.

Name ____________________

Name ______________________________

Color the heart next to each child who is loving like Jesus.

Family Time

Chapter 5: God Made My Church Family

In this lesson the children learned that the Church is God's family and that every member is important. They heard that Church members follow Jesus and try to love as he did. They know that priests serve the Church, the saints are members who are in heaven, and Mary is God's mother and theirs too. Ask your child to explain the photo frame he or she made.

Your Child

Children should know that the people they love who have died are in heaven with God and continue to care for their loved ones. Give your child a sense of belonging to the parish by introducing him or her to the priests and parishioners.

Reflect

Jesus said, "Everyone will know you are my followers, if you love one another." (adapted from John 13:35)

Pray

Jesus, help us love others as you taught.

Do

- Display a picture of Mary or set up a shrine in her honor.
- Share with your child what Mary means to you.
- Take your child to parish activities.
- Read to your child *The Relatives Came* by Cynthia Rylant. Discuss how all members of a family are important to one another. Thank God for making us part of the Church family.

For more family resources, refer to the Family Activity Booklet and visit **www.loyolapress.com/preschool.**

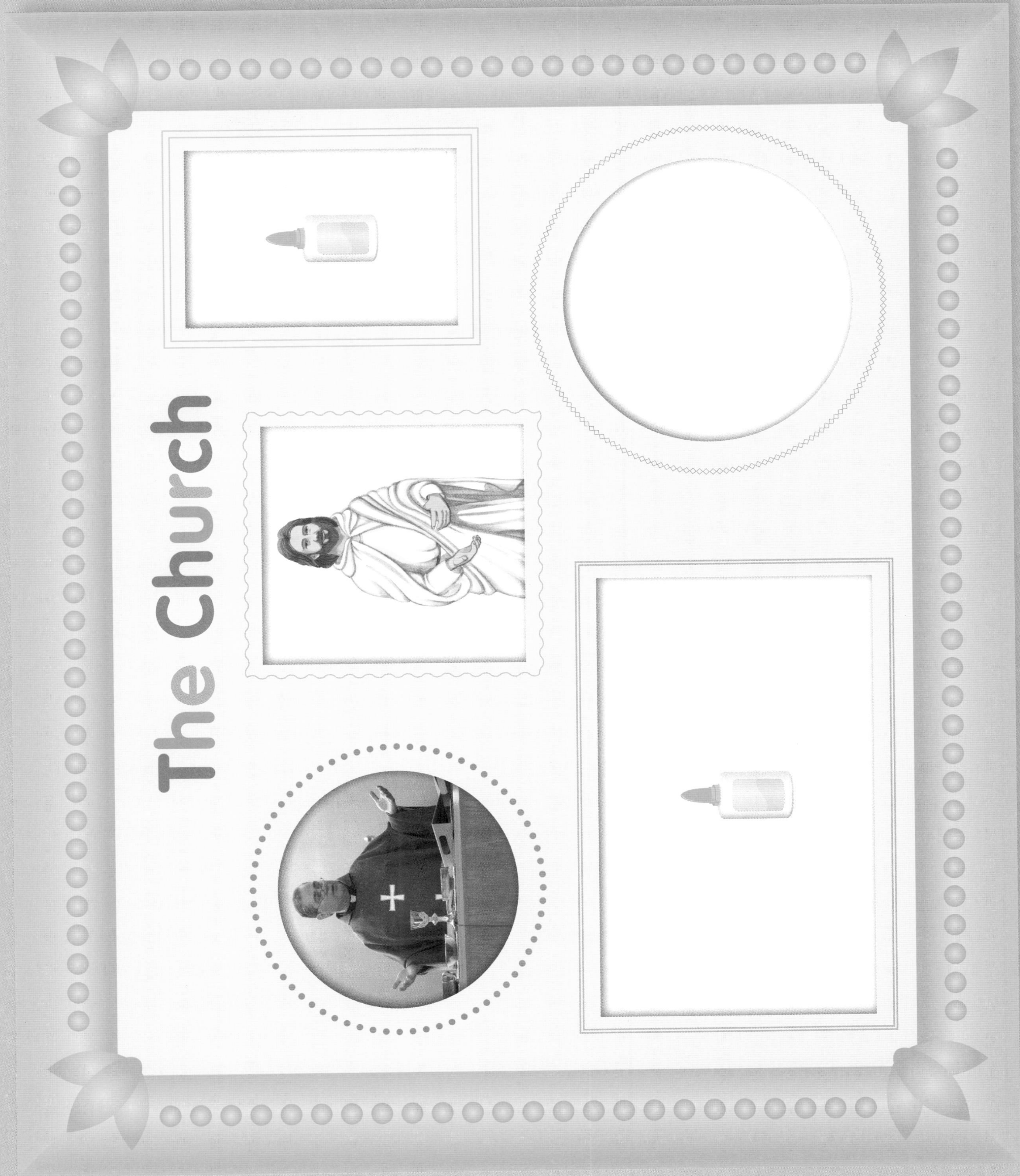
The Church

Name________

Name ________________________________

Connect the dots to finish the pictures.

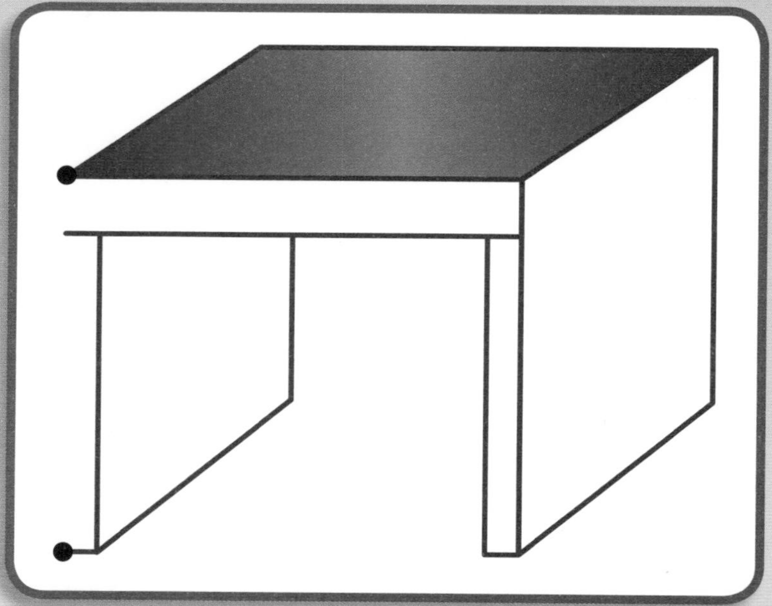

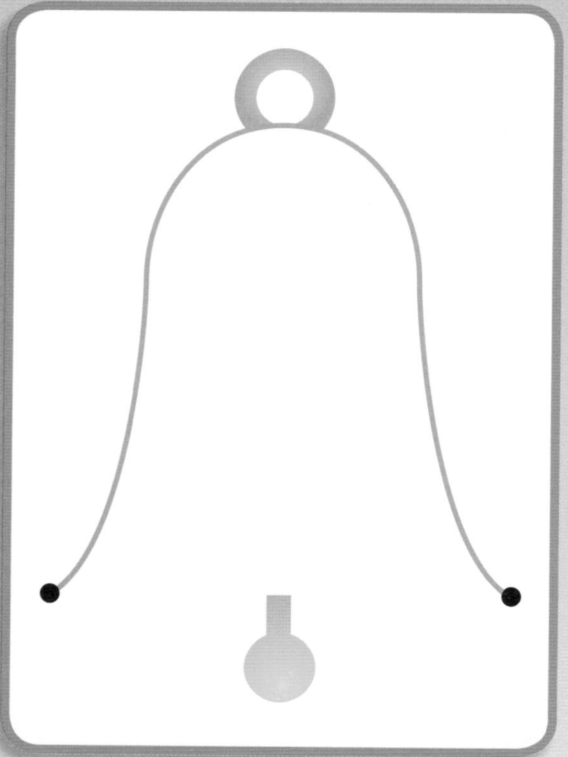

Family Time

Chapter 6:
God Made Churches

In this lesson the children became familiar with the church building and its furnishings. They learned about being quiet in God's presence and about standing and kneeling straight when we talk to God. Ask your child to tell you about the church he or she made.

Your Child

Children can feel at home in God's house at an early age. Take your child with you when you worship in church. To enable your child to see the altar, sit in the front or have your child sit on the aisle.

Reflect

I am glad when I go to God's house.
(adapted from Psalm 122:1)

Pray

God, may we worship and praise you with joyful hearts.

Do

- Make a special trip to church with your child to study some of its various features: the altar, the cross, the stained-glass windows, the candles, and so on.
- As you travel, point out different churches to your child.
- Before bedtime have your child spend a minute speaking to God quietly in his or her heart.
- Display a crucifix in your home.
- Read to your child *A Peek Into My Church* by Wendy Goody and Veronica Kelly. Talk about the special things you see in your parish church. Pray together in thanks for God's house and God's family.

For more family resources, refer to the Family Activity Booklet and visit **www.loyolapress.com/preschool.**

INRI

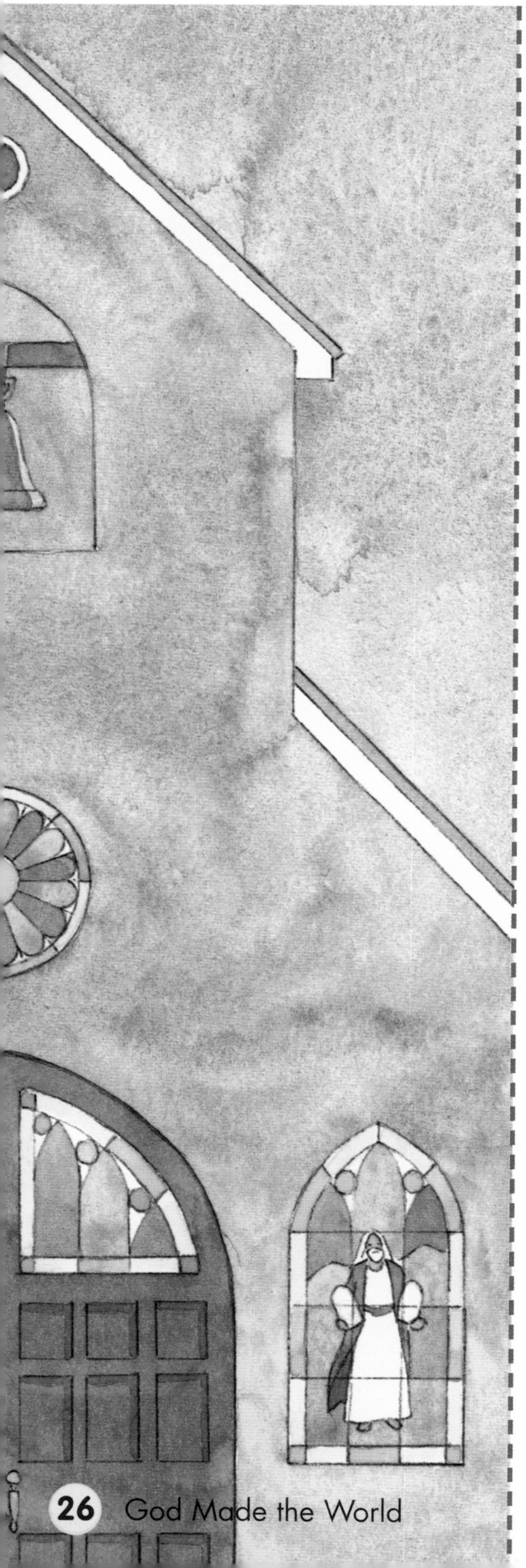

Name ______________________________________

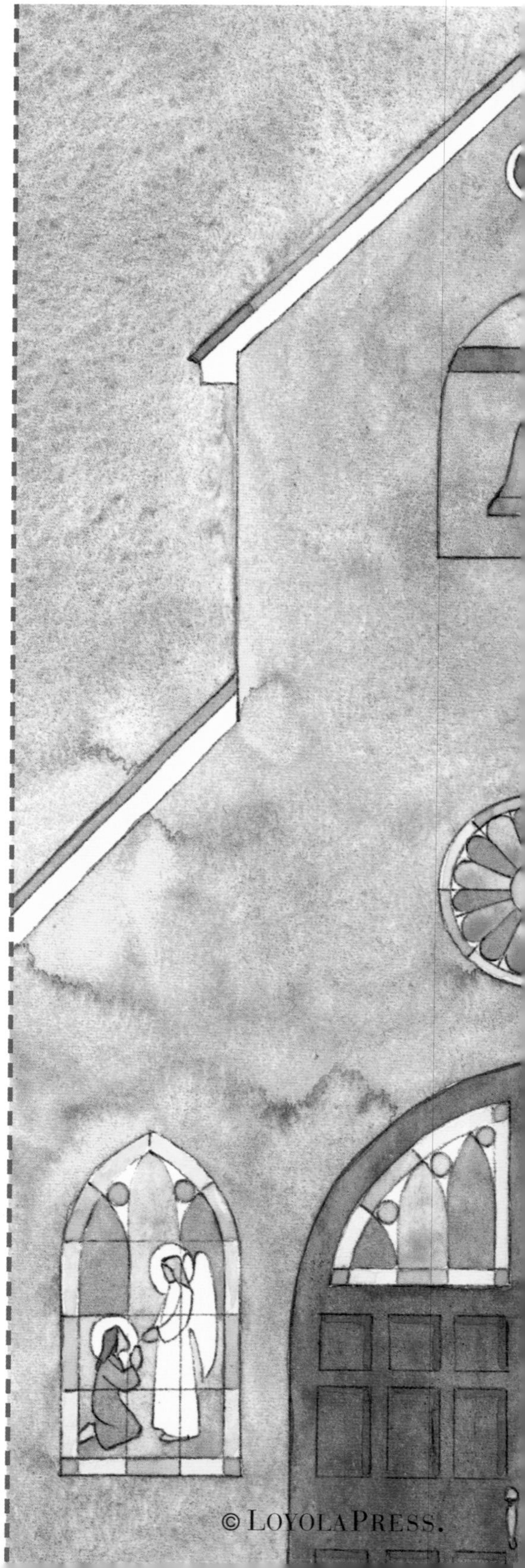

Name ______________________________

Draw yellow light around David to show that God is with him.

Family Time

Chapter 7:
God Made the Bible

In this lesson the children learned that the Bible is the Word of God in which God tells us over and over, "I love you." They learned how we show reverence for Sacred Scripture. They listened to the famous biblical story of David and Goliath. Ask your child to explain to you the prayer book he or she made. Use it to pray with your child.

Your Child

The Bible contains our Sacred Tradition and stories. Although much of the Bible is beyond the comprehension of children and not suitable for them, they ought to be exposed to what they can understand, for it is God's Word to them too. Tell your child Bible stories and verses that pertain to his or her life. For example, if your child is afraid of the dark, quote God's reassuring words in Isaiah, "Do not be afraid; I am with you." (adapted from Isaiah 41:10)

Reflect

Your word is a lamp for my feet,
a light for my path. (Psalm 119:105)

Pray

God, open our hearts to your loving Word.

Do

- Show your child the family Bible. (If you don't have a family Bible, this would be a good time to purchase one.)
- Establish a family tradition of reading the Bible together for a few minutes at least once a week, perhaps before or after a meal or on Sunday.
- Read to your child *Tomie dePaola's Book of Bible Stories* by Tomie dePaola or read from a children's Bible. Talk about why the Bible is special. Pray together, giving thanks for God's Word.

For more family resources, refer to the Family Activity Booklet and visit **www.loyolapress.com/preschool.**

God
Heaven

To: ______________________

Airmail

Dear: ____________

God

I love you.

My Prayer Book

Name ______________________________

I praise you.

2

I thank you.

3

Name ____________________

Draw strings on the harp by connecting the dots.

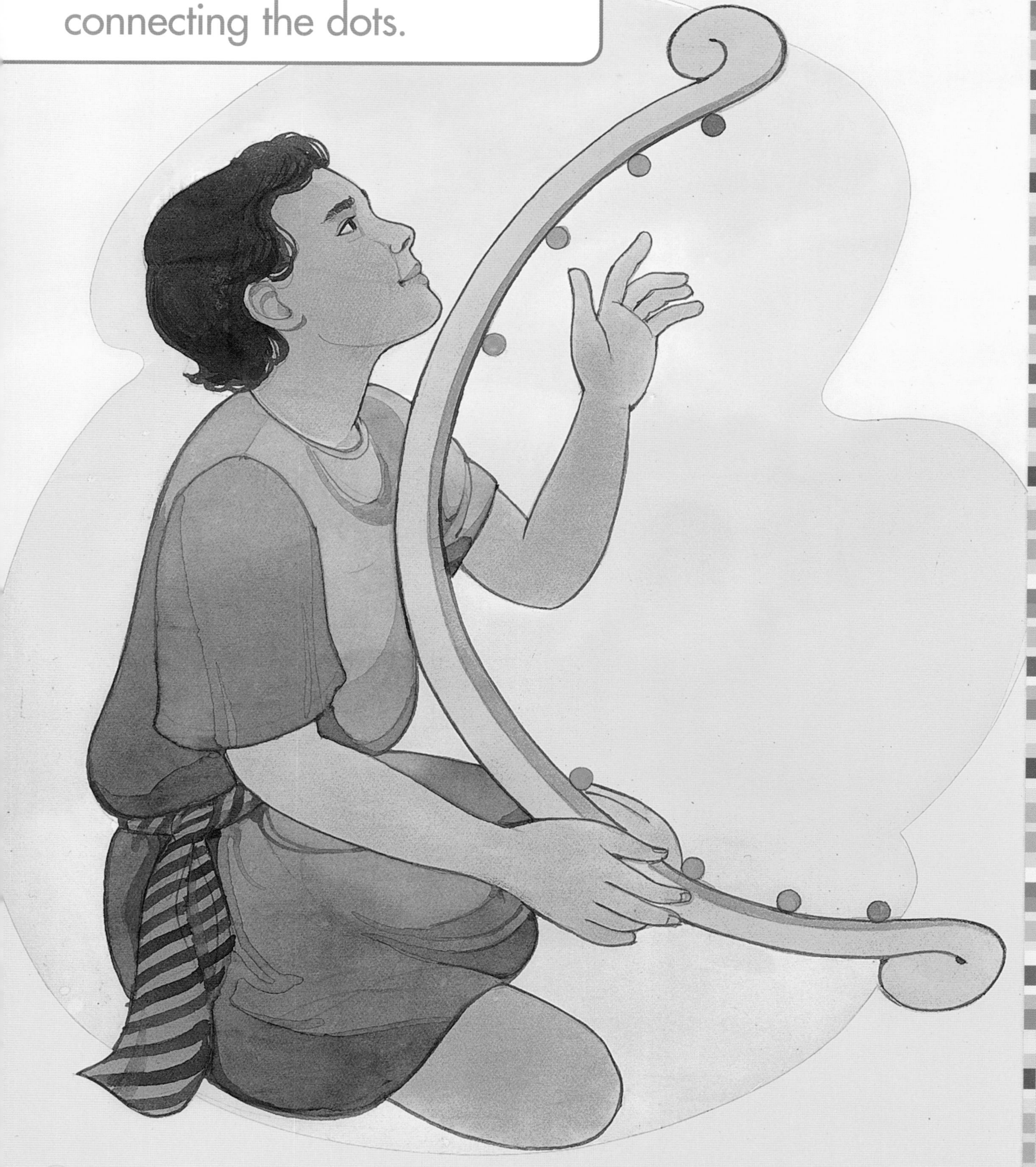

Family Time

Chapter 8:
God Made Music

In this lesson the children were led to appreciate the gift of music and to understand that we praise God with music. They sang and danced. They learned that David sang and danced and wrote songs that are in the Bible. Ask your child to show you the banner that he or she made.

Your Child

Develop your child's love of music. Play different kinds of music in your home. Think about arranging for your child to learn to play an instrument or to take dancing lessons.

Reflect

Sing to the Lord a new song. Sing joyfully to the LORD, all the earth.
(adapted from Psalm 98:1,4)

Pray

Gracious God, may we sing your praises with joy forever.

Do

- Teach your child some of the Mass responses that are sung in your parish.
- Take your child to various Masses at which different kinds of music are sung.
- Help your child memorize this adaptation of Psalm 98:1,4, which was read aloud: "Sing to the LORD a new song. Sing joyfully to the LORD all the earth."
- Go to a concert with your child.
- Read to your child *The First Song Ever Sung* by Laura Krauss Melmed. Ask your child to name or sing some favorite songs. Choose a song or hymn to sing together as a prayer to God.

For more family resources, refer to the Family Activity Booklet and visit **www.loyolapress.com/preschool.**

Name ______________________________

Name ______________________________

Draw lines to match the pictures that go together.

Family Time

Chapter 9:
God Made Water

In this lesson the children were led to be grateful for water. They talked about the many ways this gift of creation serves us. They learned that holy water is used in church and for Baptism. Ask your child to tell about the pictures on page 37. Display the picture your child made.

Your Child

The children are not too young to learn to be careful with God's gifts. Talk to your child about not wasting water and helping make lakes and streams clean.

Reflect

On the last and greatest day of the feast, Jesus stood up and exclaimed, "Let anyone who thirsts come to me and drink." (John 7:37)

Pray

Jesus, thank you for saving us through the water of Baptism.

Do

- Take your child to an ocean, lake, river, or swimming pool. Together enjoy playing in the water or just sitting or walking near it.
- Serve drinks made with water, such as lemonade or ice tea.
- Teach your child to save water in small ways, such as not letting it run while brushing his or her teeth.
- Bless your child at night by making the Sign of the Cross on his or her forehead.
- Read to your child *Why Should I Save Water?* by Jen Green. Invite your child to tell a fun story about water. Thank God for the wonderful gift of water.

For more family resources, refer to the Family Activity Booklet and visit **www.loyolapress.com/preschool.**

Name ______________________

Name ______________________________

Color the centerpiece on the table.

Family Time

Chapter 10:
God Made Food

In this lesson the children reflected on the gift of food. The foundation was laid for the gift of the Eucharist. The children talked about having meals of celebration and feeding those who are poor. Ask your child to tell you about the book he or she made. Set the place mat made by your child on your table or save it for Sunday meals.

Your Child

Children respond to the needs of others. They should learn about those who are hungry and should want to help them.

Reflect

The earth is full of the goodness of the LORD. (adapted from Psalm 33:5)

Pray

Bless us, O Lord, and these your gifts which we are about to receive from your bounty through Christ our Lord. Amen.

Do

- Begin or renew the custom of praying before meals. You might pray the Grace Before Meals shown above.
- Let your child help you make his or her favorite meal.
- Have your child help choose food to donate to those who are poor.
- Invite your child's friends for a meal.
- Begin using a certain serving plate for special family meals.
- Make dinner pleasant by having each person tell good news.
- Read to your child *The Pigeon Finds a Hot Dog!* by Mo Willems. Ask your child to name some favorite foods and talk about how each is made. Thank God for giving us good food to eat.

For more family resources, refer to the Family Activity Booklet and visit **www.loyolapress.com/preschool.**

Thank you, God.

Name ____________________

Flour is used to make
many good things.

The Story of Flour

A farmer plants seeds.

The seeds grow into wheat.

Name ______________________________

The farmer cuts the wheat.

2

The wheat goes to a mill
where it is ground into flour.

3

Name ____________________

Trace the path. Start at the bottom.

Family Time

Chapter 11:
God Made Land

In this lesson the children learned about land and some of its features: mountains, valleys, rivers, and deserts. They heard that Jesus loved the earth, and they talked about caring for it. Ask your child about the earth mobile he or she made. Hang the mobile in your child's room or in another room in your home.

Your Child

Instill in your child a reverence and respect for the earth. When you and your child see striking scenery, make a comment such as "Isn't God wonderful to give us fields that beautiful?" Point out how your family can help preserve the earth and keep it—or make it—clean and beautiful.

Reflect

[T]he Lord is the great God,
the great king over all gods,
Whose hand holds the depths of the earth;
who owns the tops of the mountains.
The sea and dry land belong to God,
who made them, formed them by hand.
(Psalm 95:3–5)

Pray

Holy Spirit, teach us to care for the earth.

Do

- Begin a postcard collection.
- Work a jigsaw puzzle of a nature scene.
- Make recycling a regular practice at home.
- Care for your lawn and garden as a family.
- Let your child help care for your home by dusting or straightening things.
- Help your child decorate your sidewalk with chalk.
- Read to your child *Where the Forest Meets the Sea* by Jeannie Baker. Talk about ways to care for the earth. Thank God for all of the earth's gifts.

For more family resources, refer to the Family Activity Booklet and visit **www.loyolapress.com/preschool.**

Name ____________________

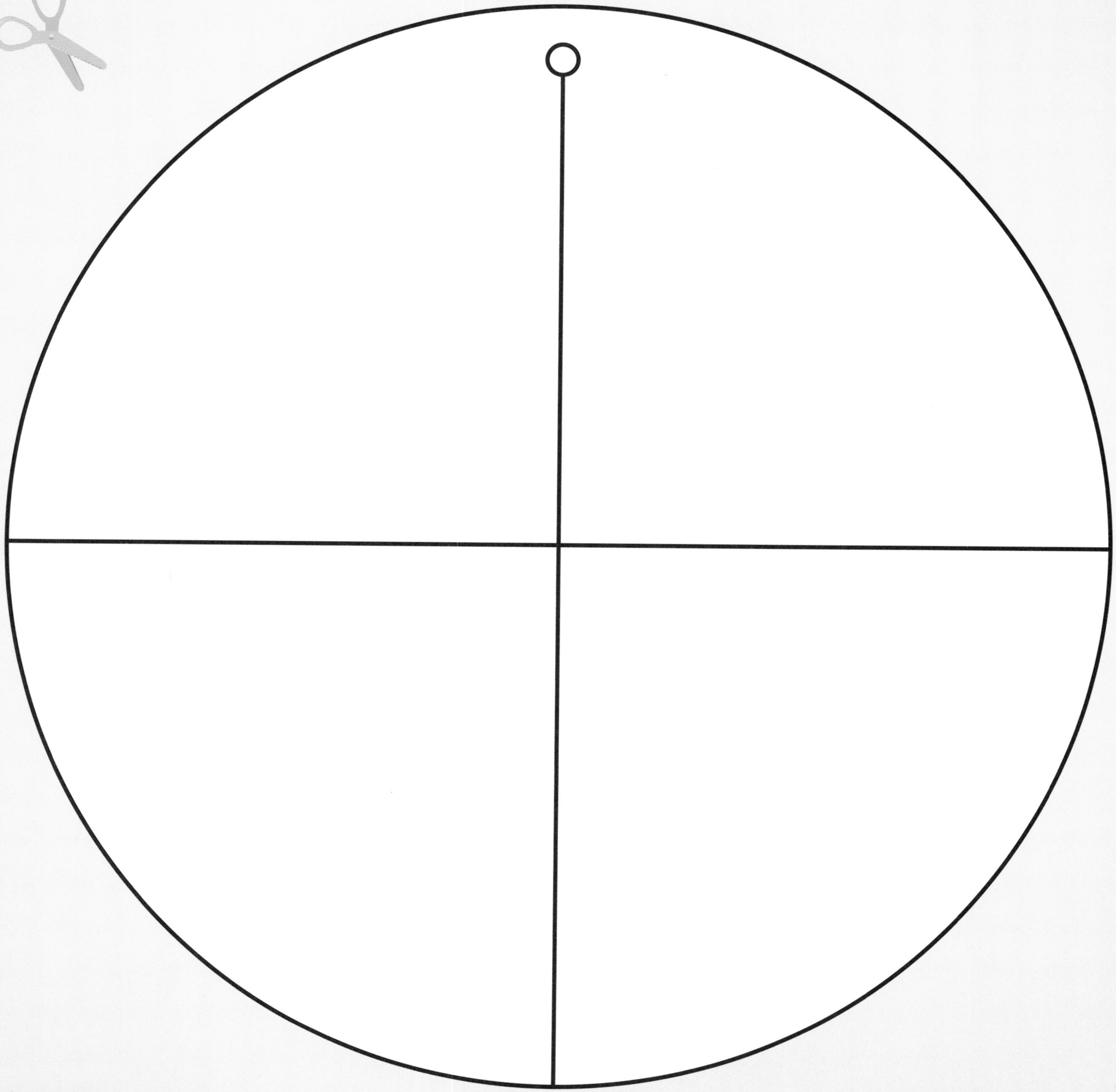

Name ______________________________

Finish the toys by tracing the gray lines.

Family Time

Chapter 12:
God Made Air

In this lesson the children learned about air and how it works for us. They heard the biblical story of the creation of human beings and how God breathed into us to give us life. Ask your child to tell you how air is like God. Praise the kite your child made.

Your Child

Children find comfort in the thought that God is everywhere. Remind your child frequently that God is always with him or her.

Reflect

The LORD God formed man out of the clay of the ground. Then God blew breath into the man, and the man came to life.
(adapted from Genesis 2:7)

Pray

God, thank you for giving us life.

Do

- On a windy day, go outside with your child and run.
- Enjoy flying a kite, blowing bubbles, or playing a kazoo with your child.
- Blow up balloons and play with them: stretch the mouthpiece to make noise as the air is released, let the balloons go and watch them fly around the room, sit on balloons to make them pop, or tie balloons to your ankles and those of your child and then try to break each other's balloons.
- Have your child listen to his or her breathing and thank God for the gift of life.
- Read to your child *Gilberto and the Wind* by Marie Hall Ets. Recall times you have observed the effects of the wind. Thank God for the gift of air that gives us life.

For more family resources, refer to the Family Activity Booklet and visit **www.loyolapress.com/preschool.**

Name ____________

Name ______________________________

Color the picture of Jesus healing the blind man.

Family Time

Chapter 13:
God Made Light

In this lesson the children learned about the gift of light. They heard the story of the healing of the blind man and know that Jesus is like light for us. They recalled that candles are used in church. Ask your child why Jesus is like light. Display your child's baptismal candle in your home, perhaps on the dining room table or on a mantelpiece.

Your Child

Light is a strong religious symbol. Whenever you can, compare light with goodness and knowledge for your child. Then he or she will be better able to understand the meaning of Christ our Light.

Reflect

Then God said, "Let there be light," and there was light. God saw how good the light was. (Genesis 1:3–4)

Pray

God, we praise you for your gift of light.

Do

- Take your child to look at a sunrise. Praise God for it, and then share a breakfast—perhaps eggs sunny-side up.
- Teach your child to make animal shadows on the wall with his or her hands.
- Show your child his or her baptismal candle and talk about how people in God's family are to be light, as Jesus is light.
- Sit in a dark room. Light a candle, nightlight, or flashlight and talk with your child about how it changes the room.
- Make a list of the lights in your home, including the sunlight playing on the walls.
- Read to your child *Sun Bread* by Elisa Kleven. Take turns naming why the sun is important to us. Praise God for the gift of light.

For more family resources, refer to the Family Activity Booklet and visit **www.loyolapress.com/preschool.**

Name ______________________________

Color the rainbow.

Family Time

Chapter 14:
God Made Color

In this lesson the children thanked God for making the various colors. They began to learn that colors can be symbols and that colors can evoke feelings. Ask your child to tell about the book of colors he or she made.

Your Child

Introduce God's multihued world to your child by teaching him or her the names of the colors.

Reflect

Look at the rainbow! Then bless God who made it. (adapted from Sirach 43:11)

Pray

God, we praise you for making this beautiful, colorful world.

Do

- Have everyone in the family tell his or her favorite color. Help your child make a picture for each person, using that person's favorite color.
- Take a walk and find something that is the same color as each color of the rainbow.
- Give a "color party" for the neighborhood children. Have them wear their favorite colors. Make a cake decorated with a rainbow. Play games; give boxes of crayons and paints for prizes.
- Keep your child supplied with pictures and sheets of blank paper to color and paint.
- Celebrate a red day (or a day of any other color). Wear red clothes, eat red food, and set out red decorations.
- Read to your child *Harold and the Purple Crayon* by Crockett Johnson. Ask your child to name his or her favorite colors. Thank God for all of the world's colors.

For more family resources, refer to the Family Activity Booklet and visit **www.loyolapress.com/preschool.**

Colors

Name ______________________________

2

3

Name ______________________________

Draw lines from the weather to the clothes you wear in it.

Family Time

Chapter 15:
God Made Weather

In this lesson the children learned about weather. They studied the various kinds of weather God created and how each kind helps us. They were encouraged to dress appropriately for different kinds of weather. Have your child explain the weather wheel he or she made and how to use it.

Your Child

Children delight in all types of weather. Take time to look outside together during various kinds of weather and praise God for it.

Reflect

"Bless the Lord, all you works of the Lord, praise and exalt him above all forever." (Daniel 3:57)

Pray

God, we bless and praise you for the wonders of your creation.

Do

- Go for a walk on a warm, rainy day. Dress your child appropriately and let him or her splash in puddles.
- If it is snowy where you live, let your child make snow people and snow angels. Go sledding or ice skating.
- Watch a weather report on TV with your child.
- Talk about how weather changes from day to day or from hour to hour.
- Hold a rain party, a snow party, or a sunshine party.
- Take a hike in the woods or go biking with your child.
- Read to your child *The Snowy Day* by Ezra Jack Keats or *Umbrella* by Taro Yashima. Recall times your family has enjoyed different types of weather. Together praise God for weather.

For more family resources, refer to the Family Activity Booklet and visit **www.loyolapress.com/preschool.**

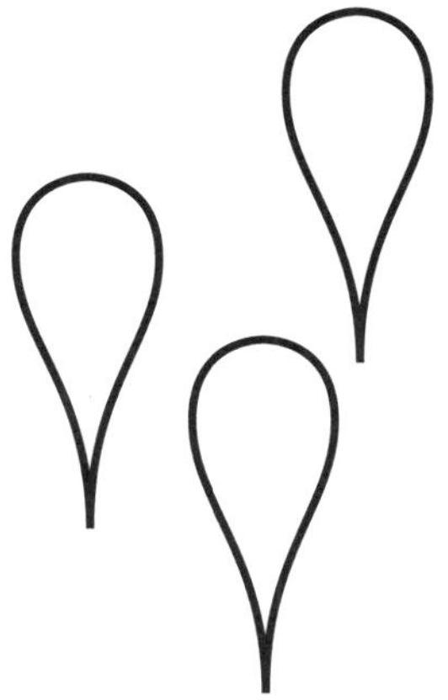

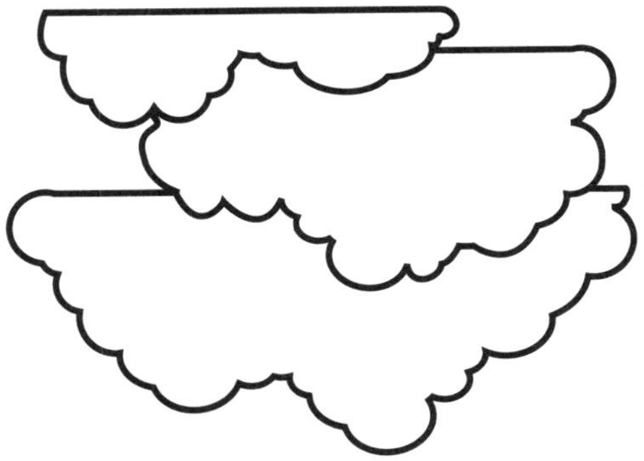

Name________________

Name ______________________________

Circle the flower that is different in each row.

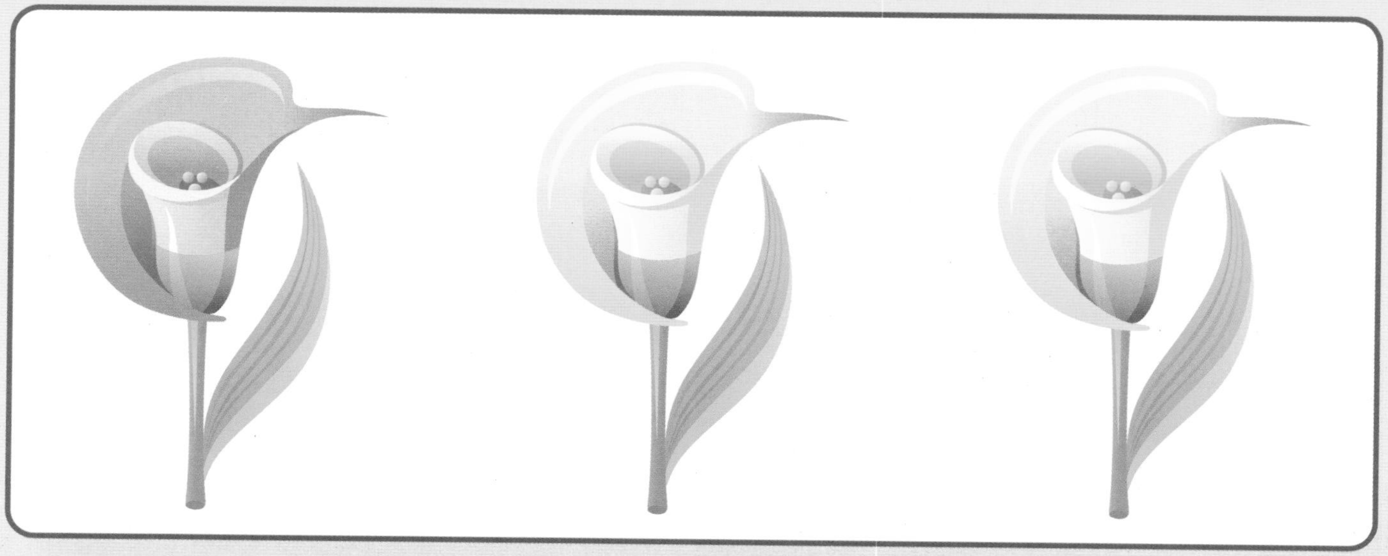

Family Time

Chapter 16:
God Made Flowers

In this lesson the children learned that flowers are a gift that expresses love. God gives us flowers, and we put flowers in church to honor God. The children reflected on the beauty of flowers and their fragrances. They heard the story of Jesus' teaching that God cares for us more than for flowers. Help your child deliver the basket of flowers he or she made to someone special.

Your Child

Cultivate a love of beauty in the heart of your child. Marvel with him or her at the wonder of flowers and their variety.

Reflect

Jesus said, "Look at the flowers. They don't work, but God clothes them in clothes more beautiful than a king's. God will take care of you just as God takes care of the flowers. You don't have to worry."
(adapted from Luke 12:27–28)

Pray

God, help us trust in your loving care.

Do

- Visit a garden or a greenhouse with your child.
- Periodically put fresh flowers on the table.
- Purchase flowers for your parish church or donate some from your garden.
- Plant flowers with your child.
- Talk to your child about how God cares for him or her.
- Read to your child *The Story of Ferdinand* by Munro Leaf. Consider the various ways people enjoy flowers. Thank God for the variety and beauty of flowers.

For more family resources, refer to the Family Activity Booklet and visit **www.loyolapress.com/preschool.**

Name ______________________________

Name ____________________

Find and circle two squirrels, two birds, a nest, and a girl.

Family Time

Chapter 17:
God Made Trees

In this lesson the children reflected on one of God's magnificent creations—trees. They talked about the many uses of trees and the role trees played in Jesus' life. They heard Jesus' teaching about a good tree bearing good fruit. Ask your child how he or she could "bear good fruit," that is, do good deeds. Show appreciation of the picture of the tree your child made.

Your Child

Children, like all of us, can be led to know God and about God through creation. Point out to your child that God is very wise to make trees, which are useful in so many ways.

Reflect

Out of the ground the LORD God made different kinds of trees grow that were delightful to look at and good for food.
(adapted from Genesis 2:9)

Pray

Jesus, make our lives bear good fruit for you.

Do

- Take a walk through the woods with your child and name different kinds of trees.
- Share together some food that came from trees: fruits or nuts or both.
- Talk about wooden things that are in your home and how they help you.
- Help your child climb a tree, sit in a tree, swing from a tree, or play in leaves.
- Read to your child *A Tree Is Nice* by Janice May Udry. Talk about why trees are important to us. Together praise God for the gift of trees and their many uses.

For more family resources, refer to the Family Activity Booklet and visit **www.loyolapress.com/preschool.**

Name ______________________________

Name ______________________________

What animals do you see in the picture?

Family Time

Chapter 18:
God Made Animals

In this lesson the children studied the wide variety of animals God created and learned how many of them help us. They also talked about caring for animals. Ask your child to tell about the animals on the animal box he or she made. Read the story "Tommy's Just-Right Pet" to your child or have him or her tell you about it.

Your Child

Reverence for all living things is something children should learn. If your child does not have a pet, you might consider getting one. Your child should share the responsibility of caring for the pet.

Reflect

God formed animals and birds out of the ground and brought them to the first man to give them names. Whatever the man called each animal was its name.
(adapted from Genesis 2:19)

Pray

God, help us care for all the animals you made.

Do

- Visit a zoo. Take pictures of various animals and make an animal photo album.
- Teach your child the names and habitats of various animals.
- Look for TV shows about animals and watch them with your child.
- Help your child become an expert on a particular favorite animal. Read aloud stories or nonfiction books about that animal.
- Read to your child *Harry the Dirty Dog* by Gene Zion. Discuss ways to care for animals. Thank God for all of the earth's animals and ask for help in caring for them.

For more family resources, refer to the Family Activity Booklet and visit **www.loyolapress.com/preschool.**

Tommy went home with the puppy and thanked God for his pet.

Tommy's Just-Right Pet

Tommy was looking for a pet. He went to a farm, and a cow said, "I'll be your pet." But Tommy said, "You would give me milk, but you need a barn."

Name ______________________________

Tommy went to the jungle, and a lion said, "I'll be your pet." But Tommy said, "You would protect me, but you would frighten the neighbors."

2

Then Tommy went down to the animal shelter. A black-and-white puppy said, "I'll be your pet." And Tommy said, "You are just right. You will be my friend. I'll take good care of you."

7

Tommy went to a forest, and a skunk said, "I'll be your pet." But Tommy said, "You are pretty, but my mother wouldn't like your perfume."

6

Tommy went to the zoo, and a giraffe said, "I'll be your pet." But Tommy said, "You would help me reach for things, but our house isn't high enough for you."

3

Tommy went to the circus, and a monkey said, "I'll be your pet." But Tommy said, "You would be fun to play with, but we have no trees for you."

4

Tommy went to the desert, and a camel said, "I'll be your pet." But Tommy said, "You would be good to ride, but your hump won't fit through our door."

5

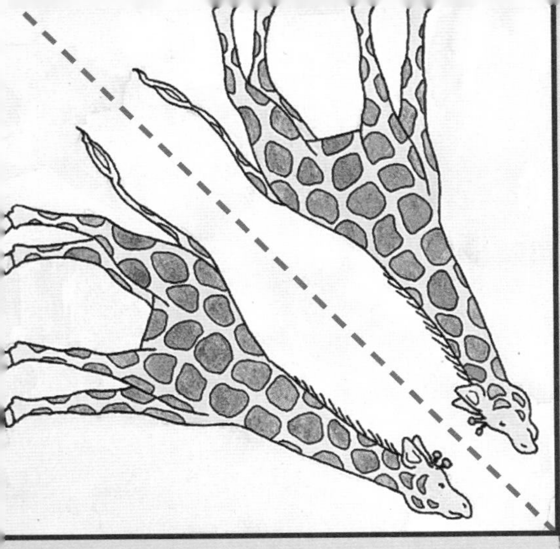

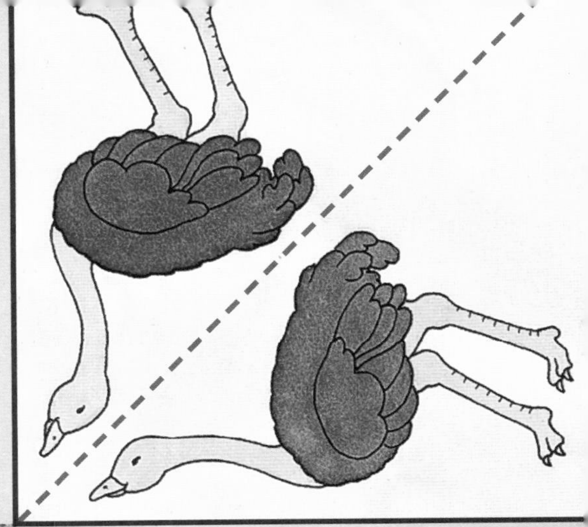

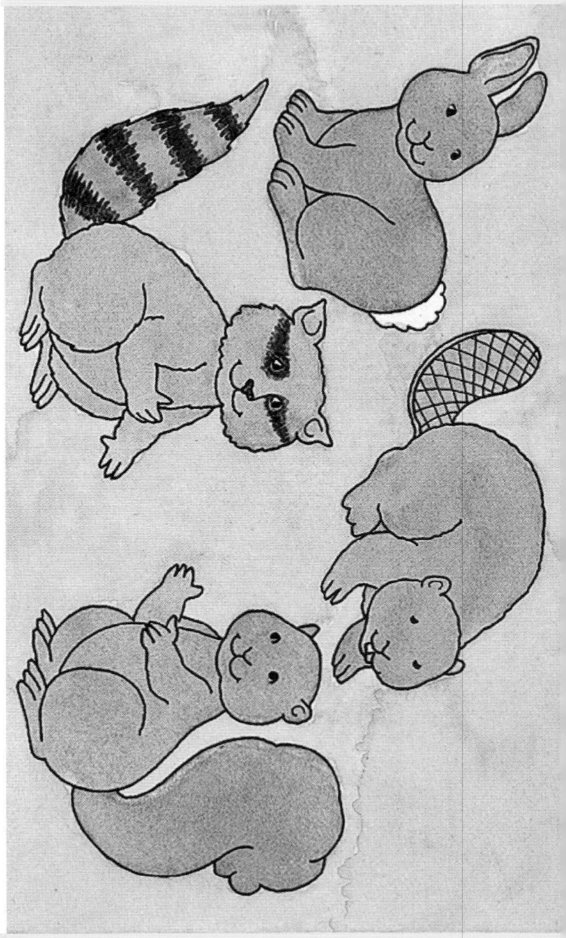

Name ________________________________

Trace the path of the mother bird to her babies.

Family Time

Chapter 19:
God Made Birds

In this lesson the children learned about birds and how our good God takes special care of them. They heard how Jesus taught us that God takes even better care of us. Help your child identify the birds on page 83. Hang in your child's room the mobile he or she made as a reminder of God's care.

Your Child

Children are fascinated by birds and for good reason. Not only can birds fly, but the relationship between the parent birds and baby birds is unique. The parents build the nest, feed the babies, and then teach them to fly. Compare the birds' care for their young with the tender care God has for us.

Reflect

[Jesus said,] "Are not five sparrows sold for two small coins? Yet not one of them has escaped the notice of God. Even the hairs of your head have all been counted. Do not be afraid. You are worth more than many sparrows."
(Luke 12:6–7)

Pray

God, we thank you for your love and care.

Do

- Let your child feed the birds in your yard or in a park. You might set up a bird feeder or birdbath and watch the birds with your child.
- Give your child binoculars to have close-up views of the birds.
- Help your child distinguish the various bird songs and birdcalls.
- Read to your child *Good-Night, Owl!* by Pat Hutchins. Consider the great variety of birds and how God cares for them. Thank God for caring for us.

For more family resources, refer to the Family Activity Booklet and visit **www.loyolapress.com/preschool.**

Name ______________________________

Name ______________________

Connect the dots that are the same color to make the net.

Family Time

Chapter 20:
God Made Fish

In this lesson the children learned about fish and other sea creatures. They praised God for these creatures. They heard the story of Jesus helping his friends catch an enormous quantity of fish. (Luke 5:1–11) Ask your child to tell you the story, using the picture on this page. Be sure to admire the picture of the fish your child made.

Your Child

The children belong to Jesus through Baptism. One spiritual writer said we are like fish in the great ocean that is God.

Reflect

Simon said in reply, "Master, . . . at your command I will lower the nets." When the fishermen had done this, they caught a great number of fish, and their nets were tearing. (adapted from Luke 5:5–6)

Pray

Jesus, help us bring others to follow you.

Do

- Enjoy a fish dinner with your child.
- Visit an aquarium or tropical fish store with your child.
- Tell your child about the day he or she was baptized and became a member of the Church. Show pictures of the event.
- Read to your child *Fish Is Fish* or *Swimmy* by Leo Lionni. Discuss the unique qualities of fish and other creatures that live in water. Praise God for the variety and beauty of fish and all the creatures of the sea.

For more family resources, refer to the Family Activity Booklet and visit **www.loyolapress.com/preschool.**

Name ______________________________

Name ____________________________

Draw a circle around the butterfly that is different.

Family Time

Chapter 21:
God Made Butterflies

In this lesson the children talked about surprises God put in our world—in particular, lovely butterflies that come from caterpillars. This prepares the children for the dramatic change we make at death when we enter into new eternal life. Have your child talk about the surprises pictured on page 91 and tell you the story of a butterfly's life. Display the picture your child made.

Your Child

The life cycle of a butterfly and the death of a seed that is born again as a flower are symbols and promises of our new life. As Jesus rose from the dead, so will we. This mystery is beyond the scope of our understanding. Answer your child's questions about death simply and honestly. Because of Jesus' Resurrection, we can rejoice in this life in preparation for the next.

Reflect

God has made a home for us in heaven.
(adapted from 2 Corinthians 5:1)

Pray

Praise the Lord, who is so good . . .
(Psalm 136:1)

Do

- Point out natural wonders, such as rainbows, to your child.
- Take your child to a natural history museum. Convey wonder over the world's marvels.
- Take a nature walk with your child and admire God's gifts.
- Plant seeds with your child and watch them grow.
- Read to your child *The Very Hungry Caterpillar* by Eric Carle. Consider the wonder of the caterpillar's transformation into a butterfly. Thank God for all the surprises in the world.

For more family resources, refer to the Family Activity Booklet and visit **www.loyolapress.com/preschool.**

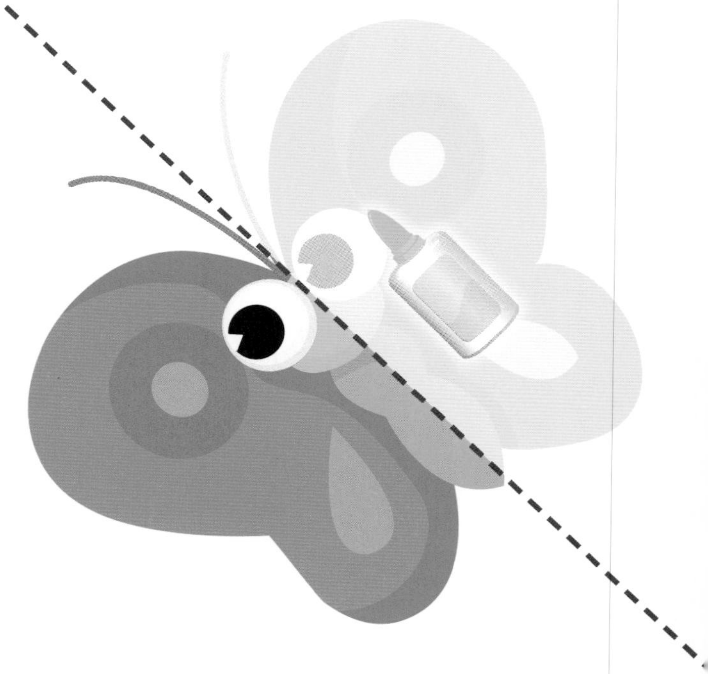

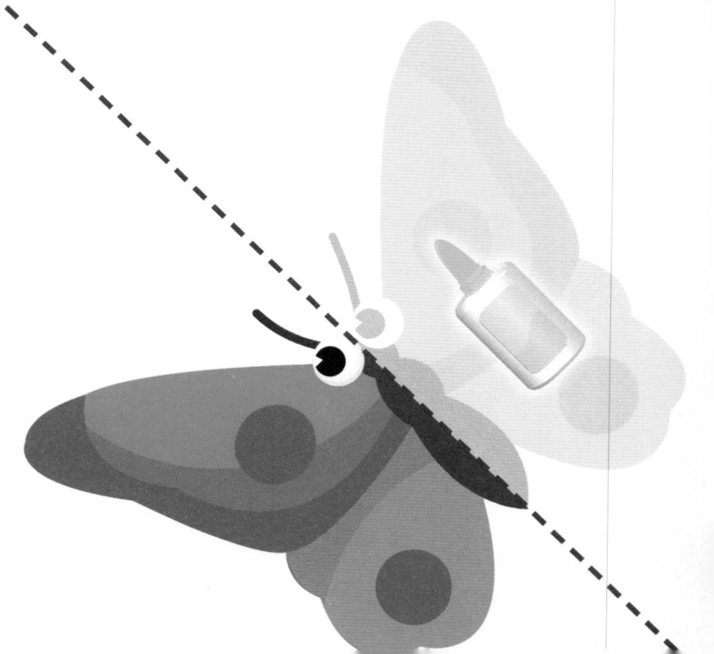

Name ____________________

Draw something you have seen that is very large.

Family Time

Chapter 22:
God Made Big Things

In this lesson the children considered some of God's huge creations, such as oceans, mountains, and elephants. They learned that God is very great and powerful. They also heard that God loves them more than these great things. Read aloud together or have your child tell you about his or her book about God's love. Ask your child to describe the giant thank-you card the group made for God.

Your Child

A valuable lesson for children is that through cooperation great things can be accomplished. Point out to your child the advantages of having a task done by a group.

Reflect

God is greater than all his works.
(adapted from Sirach 43:29)

Pray

God, we praise you for your great love.

Do

- Have your child help you make a snack or bake cookies.
- If possible, take your child where he or she can experience a large natural creation, such as a river, lake, forest, mountain, or plain.
- Help your child draw a very large picture.
- Affirm family members. Sit in a circle on the floor. Choose someone to spin a bottle and tell how God's love is shown through the person to whom the bottle points. That person then spins the bottle.
- Read to your child *The Story of Babar* by Jean de Brunhoff. Take turns naming the largest creatures and other magnificent features in the world. Praise God who is mightier than all these created things.

For more family resources, refer to the Family Activity Booklet and visit **www.loyolapress.com/preschool.**

stronger than a lion.

And God loves me!

4

My Book About God's Great Love

God's love is higher
than a mountain,

Name ________________________________

1

wider than the sky,

deeper than the ocean,

2

bigger than a whale,

3

God made . . .

Name ________________________________

Name ____________________

Circle the seven little creatures hidden in the picture.

Family Time

Chapter 23:
God Made Little Things

In this lesson the children focused on small things that God made. They learned to value small living things and praised God for them. They saw the potential of small things, such as acorns and babies. Ask your child to show you the pet pocket he or she made.

Your Child

Children can appreciate the ingenuity of the Creator by examining the intricacies of small, delicate creations. Often during walks children will stop abruptly, absorbed by some small thing.

Reflect

God looked at everything he had made and called it very good.
(adapted from Genesis 1:31)

Pray

God, help us care for all living creatures, great and small.

Do

- Study an ant or another small thing with your child. Point out its features and unique powers.
- Show your child his or her baby pictures. Call attention to the tiny fingernails and toes.
- Look at several small things through a magnifying glass with your child.
- Provide your child with a special box for collecting small treasures.
- Read to your child *The Very Quiet Cricket* by Eric Carle. Count how many small creatures your child can name. Ask God to show you ways to appreciate and care for little things.

For more family resources, refer to the Family Activity Booklet and visit **www.loyolapress.com/preschool.**

Pet Pocket

Name__________

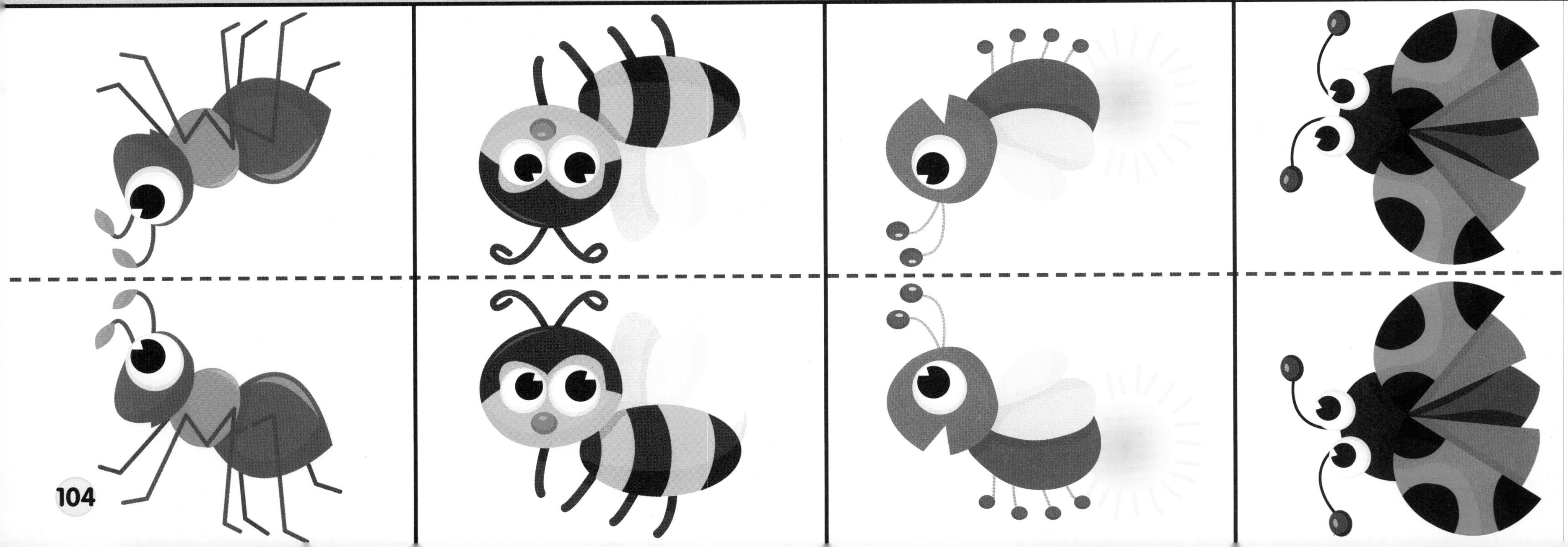

Name ______________________________

Draw a line from each child to the heart.

Family Time

Chapter 24:
God Made Countries

In this lesson the children were made aware of the many different countries that make up the world. They learned that although people in these countries may look different, eat different things, and have different customs, they are all human beings. They were led to regard others as their brothers and sisters in the family of God. Find out about the country whose flag your child made. Tell your child about it.

Your Child

Prejudice is learned quickly by children. Help your child respect other people by introducing him or her to people of different races and nationalities.

Reflect

For through faith you are all children of God in Christ Jesus. (Galatians 3:26)

Pray

Jesus, help us grow in love as brothers and sisters in God's family.

Do

- Try recipes from other countries.
- Point out to your child some accomplishments of people from other nations.
- Pray together for people in other countries who need our prayers.
- Read to your child *Whoever You Are* by Mem Fox. Ask your child to tell you what he or she knows about people who live in other countries. Ask God to bless all the people in the world.

For more family resources, refer to the Family Activity Booklet and visit **www.loyolapress.com/preschool.**

Belgium

Italy

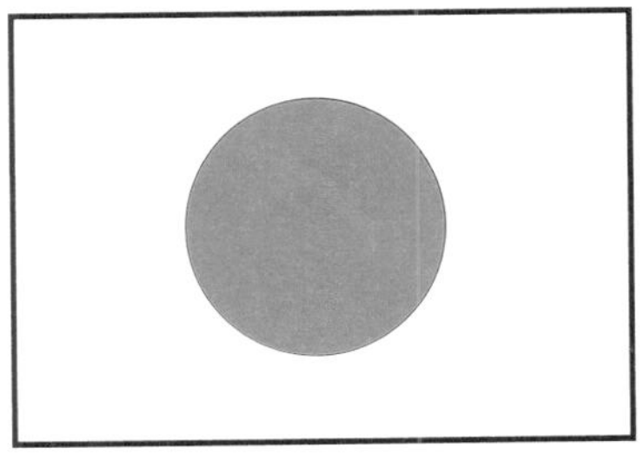

Japan

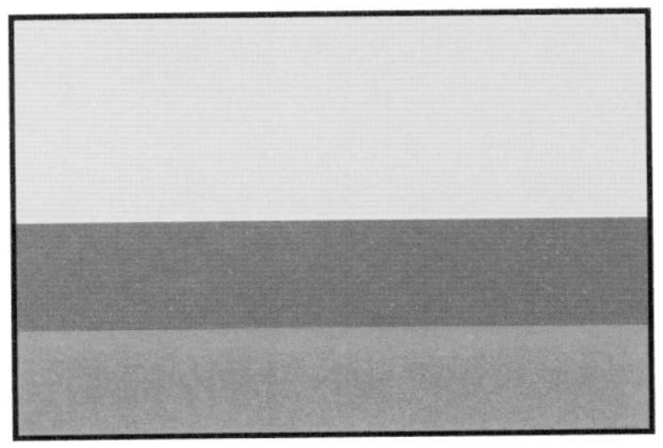

Colombia

Nigeria

Vietnam

Name ______________________________

Name ____________________

What do you think is funny?

Family Time

Chapter 25:
God Made Laughter

In this lesson the children learned that God wants us to be happy and that being close to God makes us happy. They talked about ways to make other people happy. Suggest that your child wear the party hat he or she made to show others when he or she is feeling especially happy.

Your Child

One of the best ways to be happy is to make someone else happy. Do something with your child to surprise someone and make that person happy.

Reflect

Your hearts will be happy and your joy will last forever. (adapted from John 16:22)

Pray

God, we praise you with joy now and forever.

Do

- Enjoy a comical TV program or DVD with your child.
- Share jokes with your child.
- Do something to make your child happy, such as preparing his or her favorite meal for dinner.
- Tell your child a funny story.
- Plan summer activities that would be fun for everyone in the family.
- Read to your child *Silly Sally* by Audrey Wood. Enjoy making your own silly rhymes. Praise God for the gift of joy.

For more family resources, refer to the Family Activity Booklet and visit **www.loyolapress.com/preschool.**

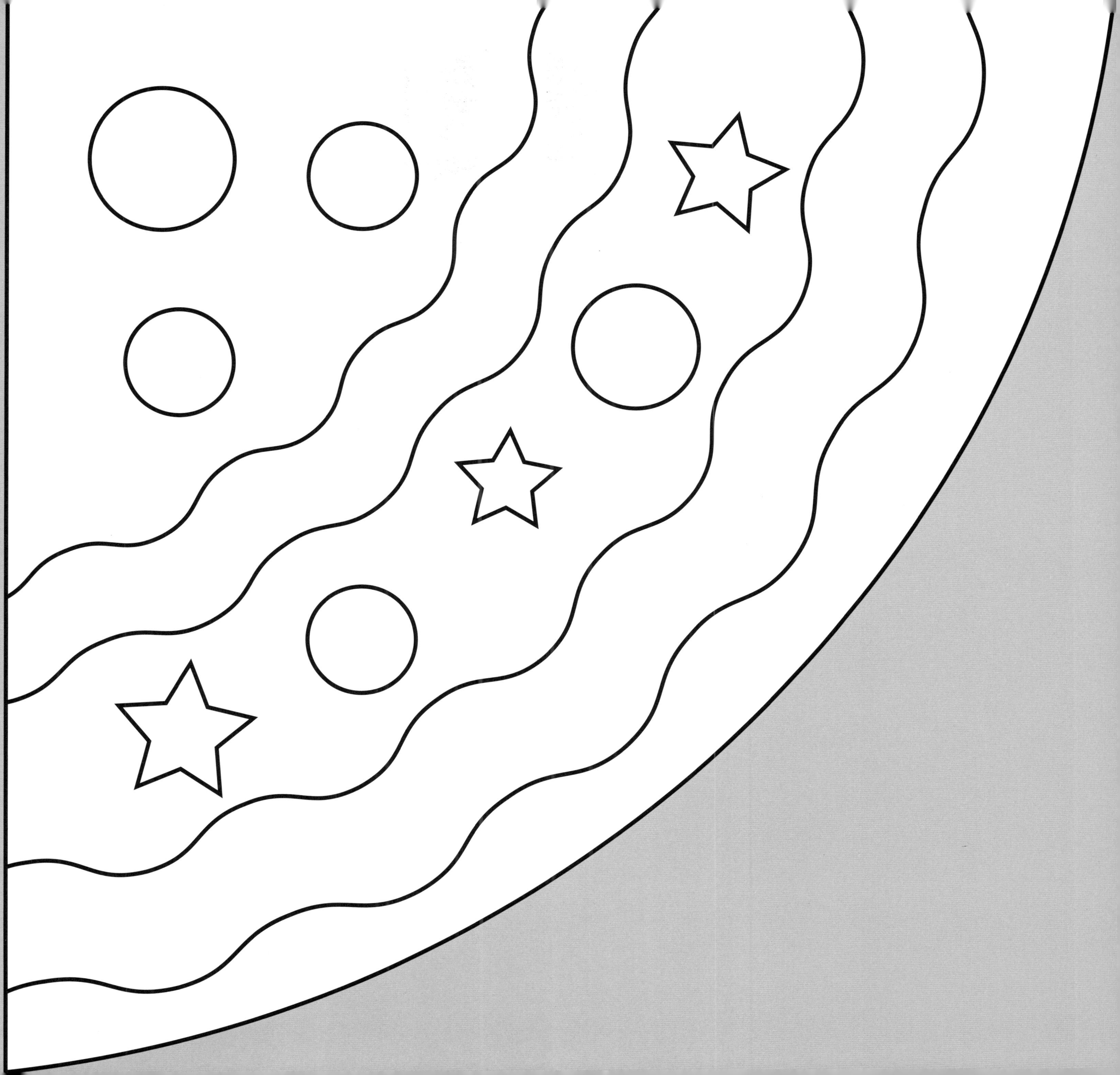

Name ______________________

Name ____________________

Color the pieces orange that have a dot.

Family Time

Special Lesson 1:
Halloween/Feast of All Saints

In this lesson the children learned that Halloween is the night before we celebrate the feast of All Saints. They heard the story of Saint Elizabeth of Hungary and were invited to let God's love shine from them as Elizabeth did. They were encouraged to show love by smiling. Ask your child why he or she made a crown.

Your Child

For children, Halloween should be a night of fun in safe surroundings. You might hold a party at your house on Halloween for your child and his or her friends.

Reflect

Jesus said, "You are the light of the world. Let your light shine so people see the good things you do and praise our Father in heaven." (adapted from Matthew 5:14,16)

Pray

Jesus, may the light of your love shine through us.

Do

- Carve a pumpkin with your child.
- Tell your child about his or her patron saint.
- Make a special bag to hold treats for your child.
- Read to your child *The Pumpkin Book* by Gail Gibbons. Talk with your child about ways to bring joy to others. Pray together, asking God to let the light of his love shine through you.

For more family resources, refer to the Family Activity Booklet and visit **www.loyolapress.com/preschool.**

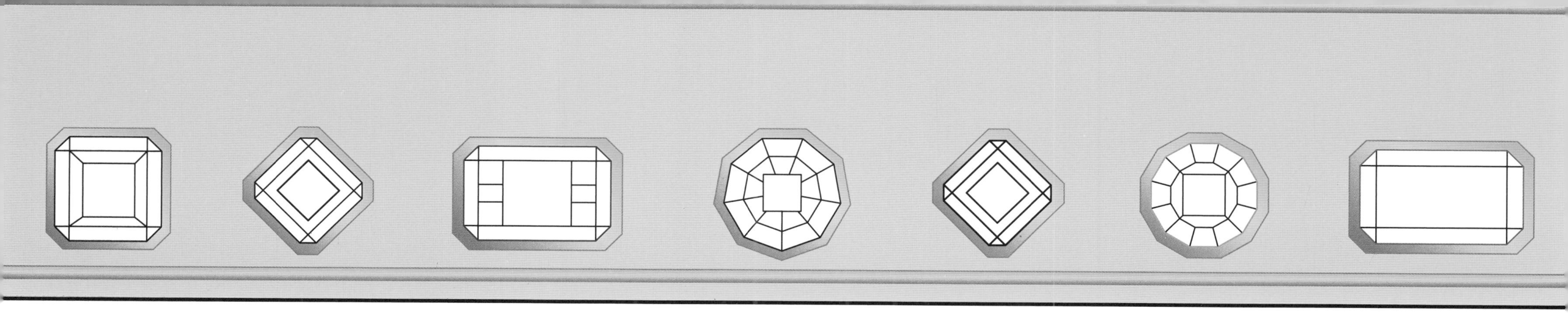

Name ____________________

Color the ★ pieces ▬ and the ● pieces ▬ .

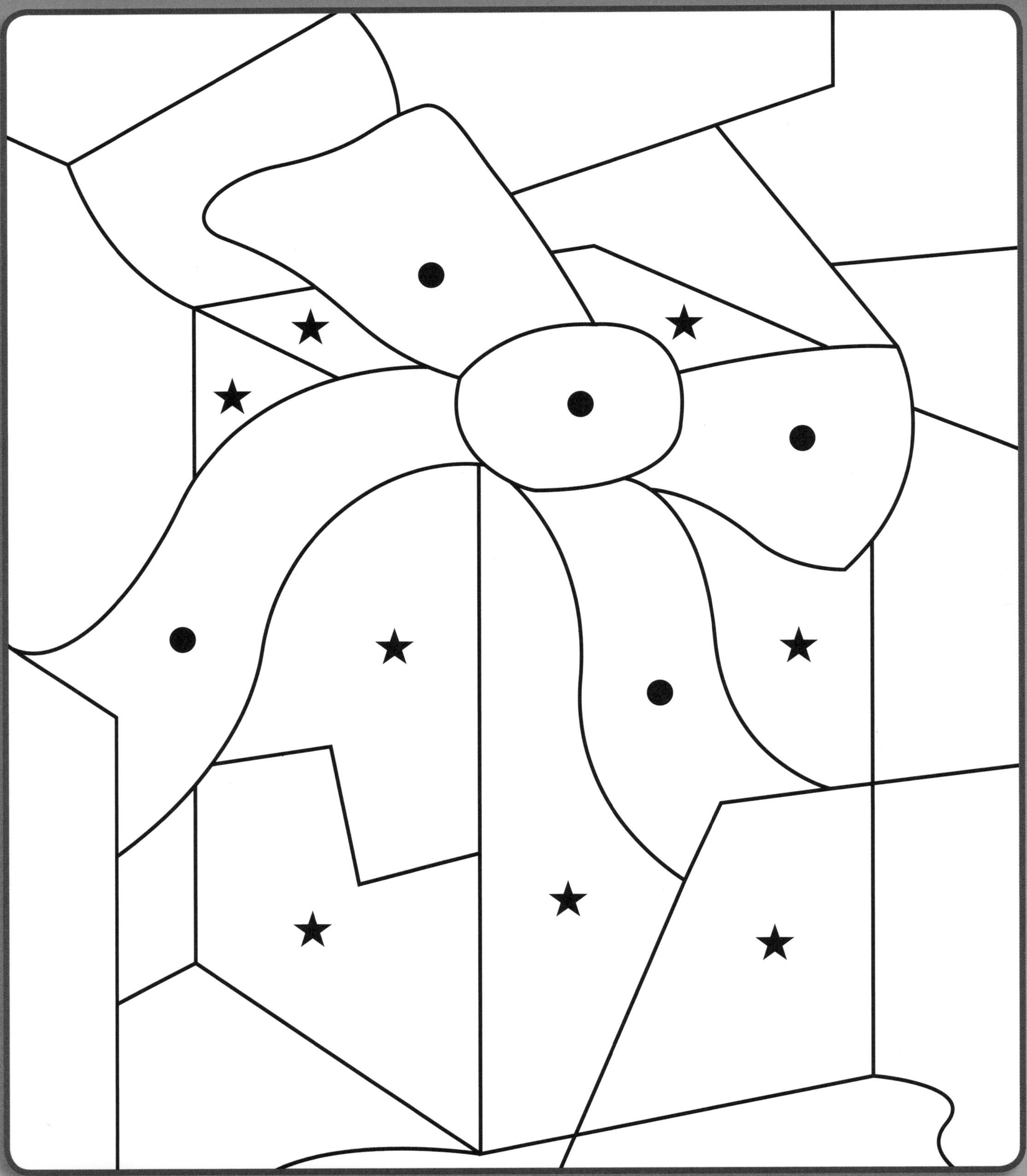

Family Time

Special Lesson 2: Advent

In this lesson the children learned that we prepare for Jesus' birthday by being kind and loving. The children made a manger and will put a piece of "straw" into it for every good act they do. Suggest acts that your child is able to do.

Your Child

Christmas is usually a child's first introduction to Jesus. Take advantage of this feast to talk about Jesus, Mary, and Joseph.

Reflect

Mary gave birth to a son, wrapped him in swaddling clothes and laid him in a manger. (adapted from Luke 2:7)

Pray

God, may we always be ready to welcome Christ into our hearts.

Do

- Set up a manger scene at home.
- Take your child with you to deliver food and clothing to people who need them.
- Join a group of Christmas carolers with your child.
- Help your child make homemade gifts for family members.
- Have a prayer service to bless your Christmas tree or manger scene. *Catholic Household Blessings & Prayers,* published by the United States Conference of Catholic Bishops, offers many ideas for family prayers, such as Christmas blessings.
- Read to your child *Waiting for Christmas: A Story About the Advent Calendar* by Kathleen Long Bostrom. Help your child count the number of days until Christmas. Pray for God's blessing as your family prepares to celebrate Christ's birth.

For more family resources, refer to the Family Activity Booklet and visit **www.loyolapress.com/preschool.**

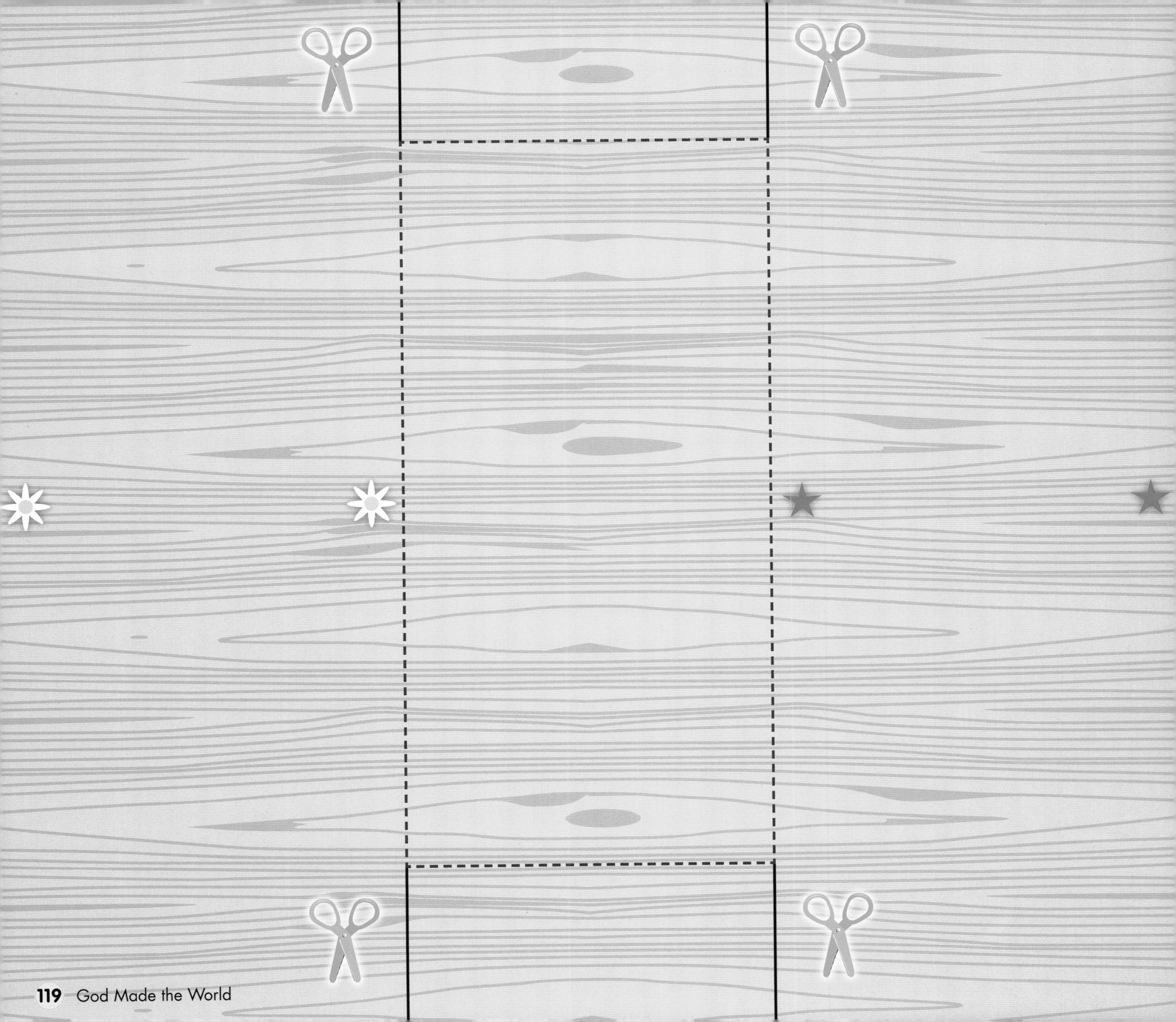

Name____________________

Name ______________________

Color the ornament.

Family Time

Special Lesson 3: Christmas

In this lesson the children heard the Christmas story. They learned that God sent Jesus into the world and that we celebrate Jesus' birthday on Christmas. The children had a procession to a representation of Jesus in a manger. Display the Christmas tree your child made.

Your Child

Stress the spiritual meaning of Christmas over the secular, materialistic meaning. Plan to take your child to Christmas Mass.

Reflect

"For today in the city of David a savior has been born for you who is Messiah and Lord." (Luke 2:11)

Pray

Jesus, your birth among us fills us with joy.

Do

- Involve your child in your preparations for Christmas: putting up decorations, decorating the Christmas tree, writing Christmas cards, making cookies.
- Pray a blessing for your Christmas tree together.
- Plan activities in which your child can give joy to others.
- Give a religious gift to your child for Christmas.
- Read aloud together the Christmas cards received each day and pray for the senders.
- Read to your child *The Friendly Beasts* by Tomie dePaola. Talk about the gifts of love that you can give to others to welcome Jesus' birth. Pray together by singing a Christmas hymn around the family Nativity set.

For more family resources, refer to the Family Activity Booklet and visit **www.loyolapress.com/preschool.**

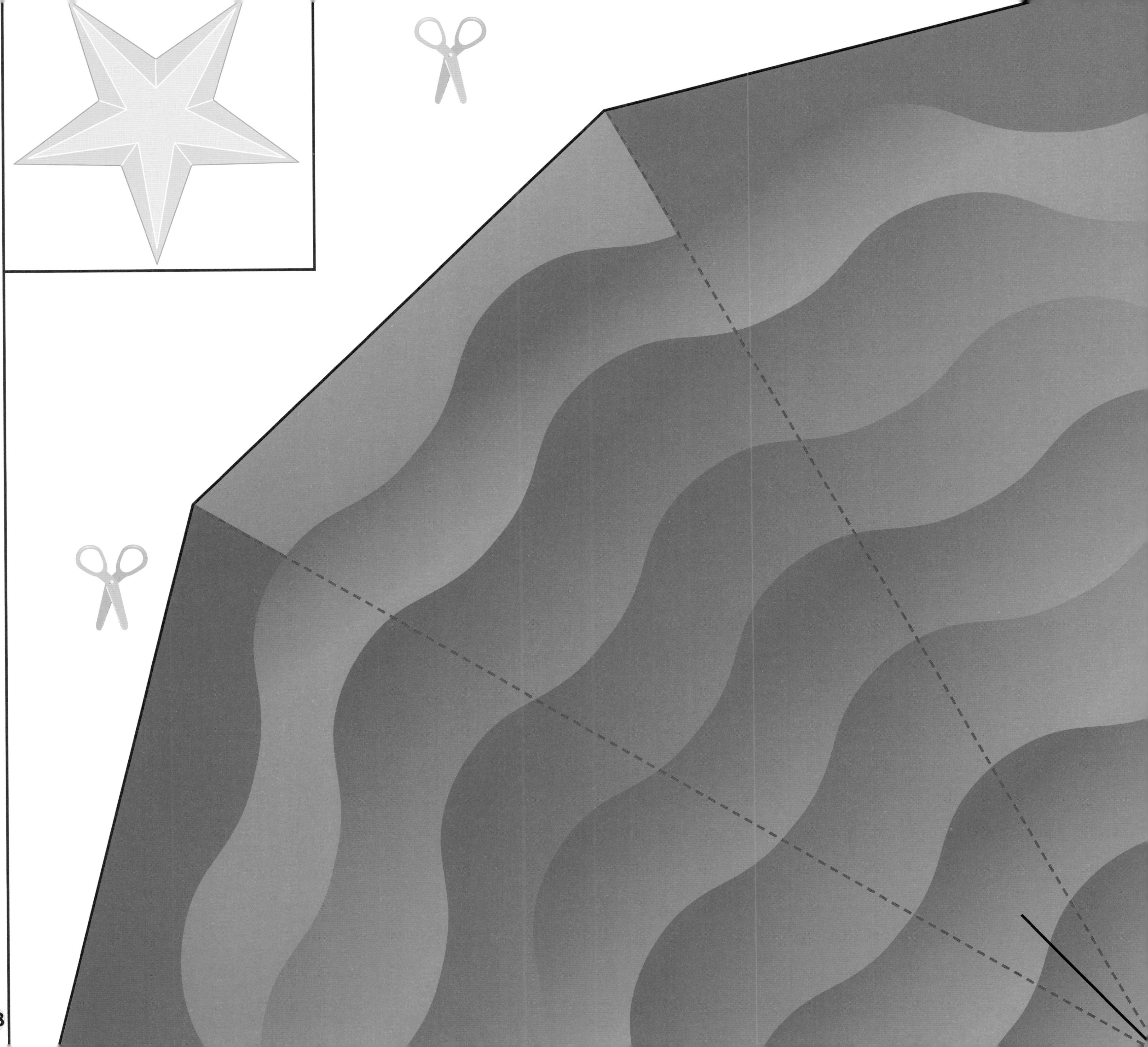

Name ______________________________

Name ________________________

Circle the pictures of people showing love to others.

Family Time

Special Lesson 4: Lent

During the season of Lent, the Church community prepares to celebrate Easter by renewing our commitment to live as Christ's disciples. In this lesson the children identified ways that we can show love to others and learned that these actions also show our love for God. They learned that we follow Jesus when we show our love for God in our words and deeds.

Your Child

Through the example of those who love and care for them, children learn the importance of showing love to others in word and action. Encourage your child's efforts to demonstrate care for others. Invite your child to participate with you in activities that show care and concern for others.

Reflect

Children, let us love not in word or speech but in deed and truth. (1 John 3:18)

Pray

Jesus, help us follow you by showing love to others.

Do

- Invite your child to draw a picture for a family member or neighbor who is ill or needs cheering up.
- Take your child grocery shopping to select food items to donate to the local food pantry.
- Choose a special prayer to say each day during Lent, such as the prayer above.
- Read to your child *My Day with Jesus* by Alice Joyce Davidson. Together choose an action to do during Lent to demonstrate your love for God and for others. Pray for God's blessing during this season of Lent.

For more family resources, refer to the Family Activity Booklet and visit **www.loyolapress.com/preschool.**

Name ________________________________

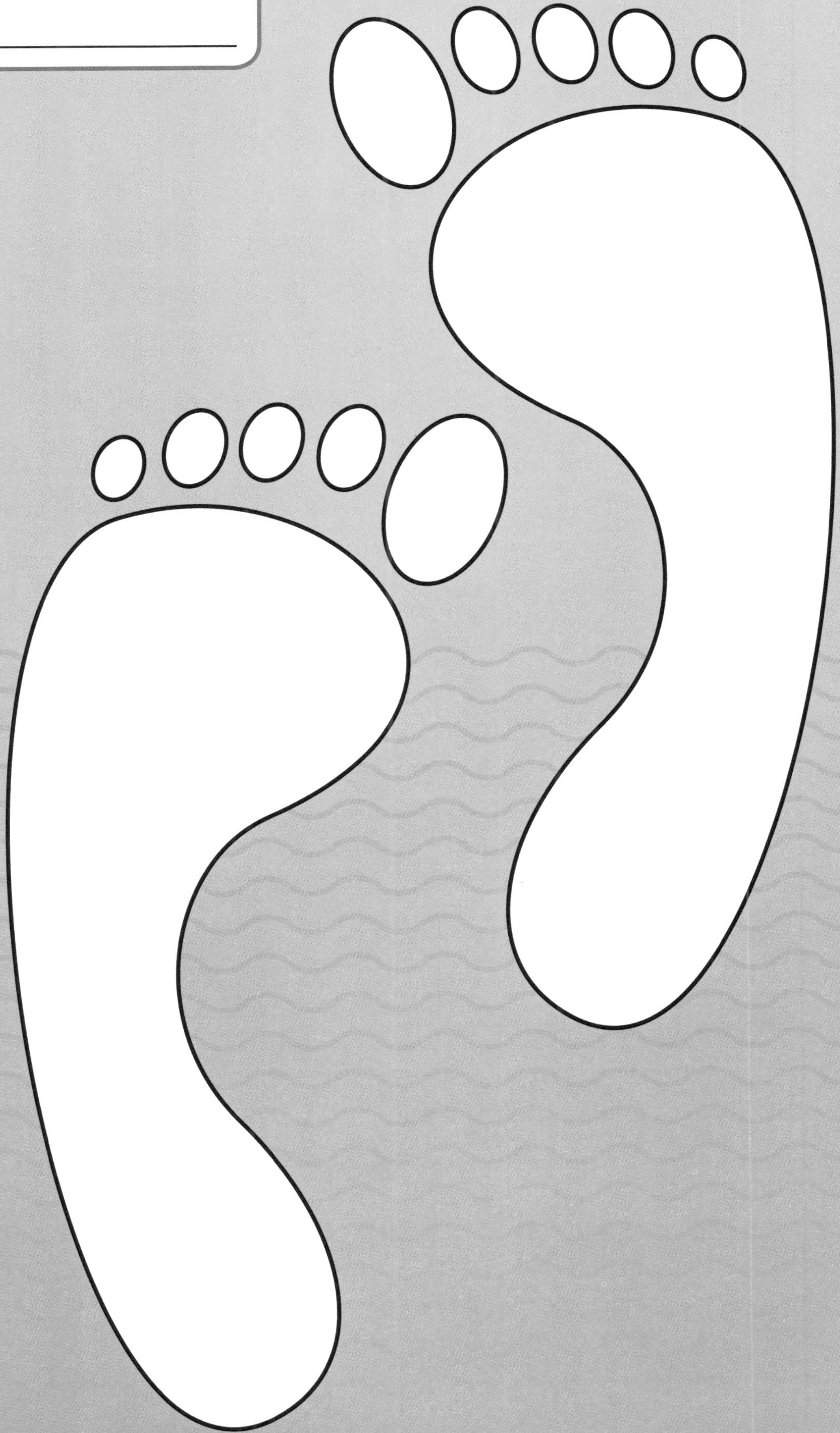

Name ____________________

Color the Easter egg.

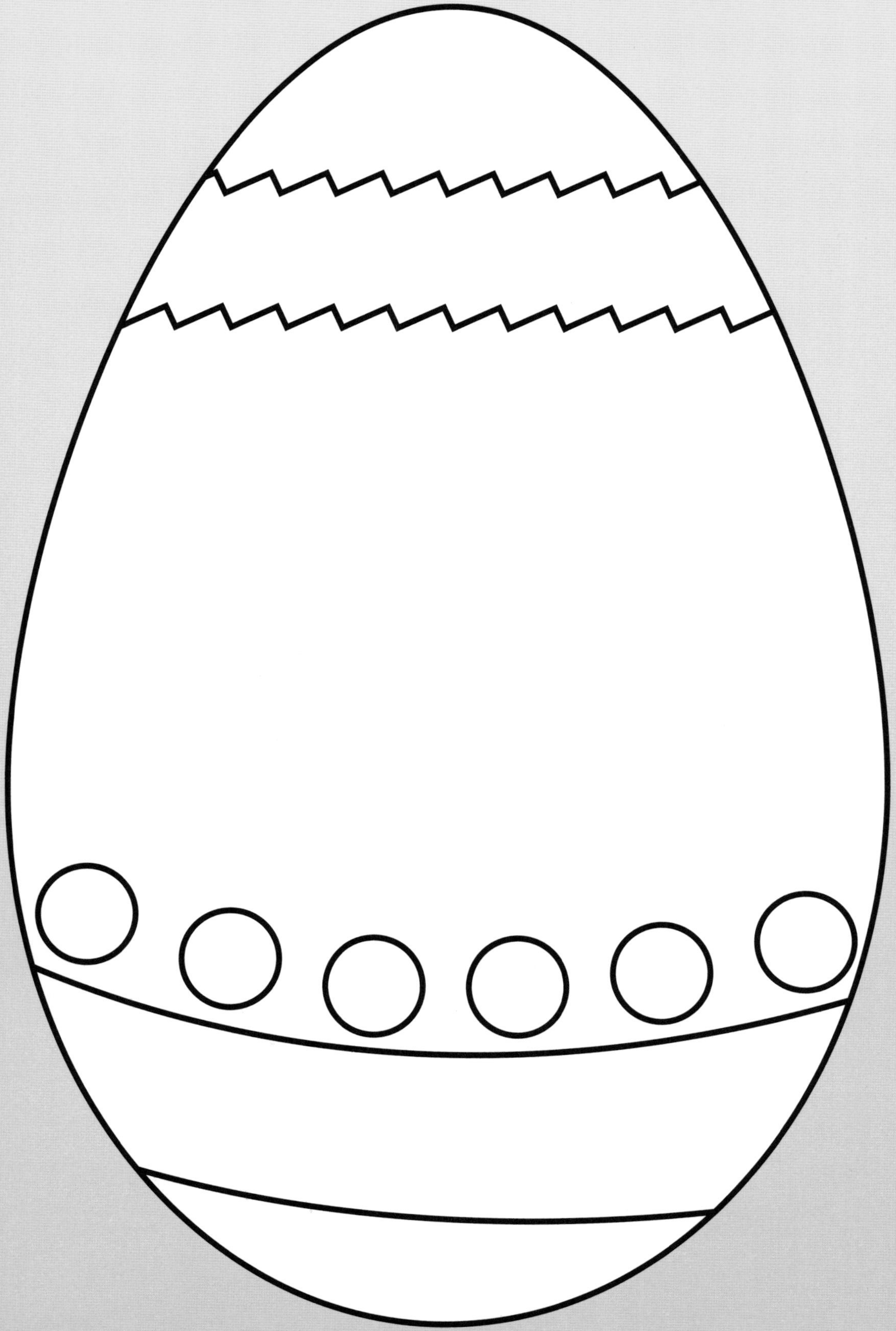

Family Time

Special Lesson 5: Easter

In this lesson the children were introduced to Easter as a celebration of life. Through the Resurrection of Jesus, we have new life and new hope. The children learned that just as the sun rises each morning, we will rise and live forever as Jesus promised us. Admire the egg your child decorated. Ask your child to explain the Easter card he or she made. Display it in your home for Easter.

Your Child

As young children experience surprise and joy at finding an Easter basket early Sunday morning, they share the emotions of the first Christians, who witnessed Christ's Easter miracle. Enjoy the beauty and freshness of the Easter season with your child. Take a walk or play in a park.

Reflect

Jesus said, "I am the resurrection and the life; whoever believes in me will live forever." (adapted from John 11:25)

Pray

Jesus, your promise of eternal life fills us with hope and joy.

Do

- Watch a sunrise with your child.
- Arrange for your child to watch a chick hatch.
- Hold an Easter egg hunt.
- Read to your child *My First Story of Easter* by Tim Dowley. Invite your child to retell the Easter story. Together praise Jesus, our risen Lord, by singing "Alleluia."

For more family resources, refer to the Family Activity Booklet and visit **www.loyolapress.com/preschool.**

Name ______________________________

Name ________________________________

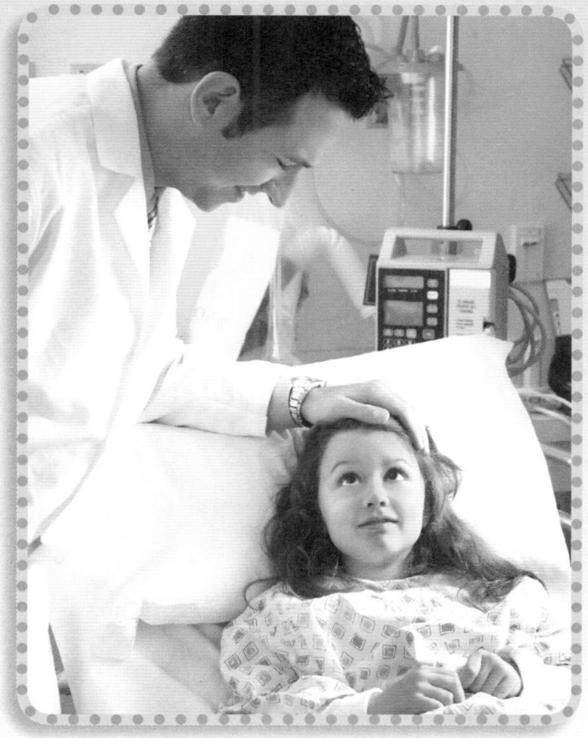

Match the pictures of people helping others by sharing peace.

Family Time

Special Lesson 6: Pentecost

On Pentecost we celebrate the gift of the Holy Spirit. In this lesson the children learned that Jesus gave his friends a helper who would be with them always. They learned that this helper, the Holy Spirit, is also with us always and brings us peace. They discussed ways to bring peace to others and practiced sharing a sign of peace. They made a wind sock for their classroom as a reminder to be peacemakers.

Your Child

Young children take comfort in knowing that God is with them always. As they are reminded of God's presence with them, they become aware of the Holy Spirit's gift of peace.

Reflect

Jesus said, "Peace be with you. Receive the holy Spirit." (adapted from John 20:19,22)

Pray

Holy Spirit, fill us with peace.

Do

- Choose an action you can take as a family to bring the Holy Spirit's gift of peace to others.
- Help your child practice sharing a sign of peace and encourage your child to participate in this part of the Mass.
- Hang a decorative flag or wind sock outside as a reminder of the Holy Spirit's gift of peace.
- Read to your child *The Very First Christians* by Paul L. Maier. Ask your child to describe what happened when the Holy Spirit came at Pentecost. Pray together, asking to receive the Holy Spirit's gift of peace.

For more family resources, refer to the Family Activity Booklet and visit **www.loyolapress.com/preschool.**

Name ________________________________

Draw something you thank God for.

Thank you, God

Family Time

Special Lesson 7: Thanksgiving

In this lesson the children learned that Thanksgiving Day is a day to thank God. They made a thank-you card for God. Incorporate the stand-up turkey your child made in your Thanksgiving Day dinner centerpiece.

Your Child

Let your child see and hear you praying in thanksgiving to God.

Reflect

Give thanks to the Lord, who is good, whose love lasts forever. (adapted from Psalm 118:29)

Pray

God, thank you for giving us so many wonderful gifts.

Do

- Invite a person to your Thanksgiving dinner who otherwise might not celebrate Thanksgiving.
- Take your child with you to deliver food or clothing to those who are poor.
- Let your child help with your Thanksgiving dinner.
- Prepare a special prayer for your Thanksgiving meal. Everyone around the table might express gratitude for one thing.
- Plan to celebrate the Eucharist as a family on Thanksgiving Day.
- Read to your child *Sometimes It's Turkey, Sometimes It's Feathers* by Lorna Balian. Talk with your child about your family's Thanksgiving traditions. Pray a litany of thanks by praying "God, we thank you" as you take turns naming things for which you are thankful.

For more family resources, refer to the Family Activity Booklet and visit **www.loyolapress.com/preschool.**

Happy Thanksgiving

Name ____________________________________

Name ____________________

Find and circle the five hearts.

Family Time

Special Lesson 8:
Valentine's Day

In this lesson the children learned that Valentine's Day is a day to show love. They talked about how to show love for other people. They made a special valentine for someone. Give your child a big hug on Valentine's Day.

Your Child

Children learn how to love in the home. God's love is usually first communicated to them through their parents. Surprise your child sometimes with hugs, kisses, and little gifts. Show appreciation for signs of love from your child.

Reflect

[Jesus said,] "As I have loved you, so you also should love one another." (John 13:34)

Pray

Jesus, help us love others as you have loved us.

Do

- Bake heart-shaped cookies with your child. Decorate them, if you wish, and take some to a neighbor.
- Help your child address and send valentine cards to friends, relatives, and helpers.
- Read to your child *Louanne Pig in the Mysterious Valentine* by Nancy Carlson. Ask your child to name ways we show love to others, on Valentine's Day and every day. Thank God for loving us always.

For more family resources, refer to the Family Activity Booklet and visit **www.loyolapress.com/preschool.**

I Love You

Name ______________________________

Name ____________________________

Circle what your mother does for you.

Family Time

Special Lesson 9:
Mother's Day

In this lesson the children pondered the many ways their mothers show love for them. They were encouraged to show love in return.

Your Child
Your child experiences God's love mainly through you, the family. Mirror God's abiding love by demonstrating your concern and care for your child. Spend some extra quality time with your child.

Reflect
Children, obey your parents in everything[.] (Colossians 3:20)

Pray
God, make strong the love between mothers and their children.

Do
- Let your child share in some of the tasks of the mother in your family: dusting, folding laundry, setting the table, planting or watering plants.
- Visit, call, or write the grandmothers in your family.
- Have a special meal in honor of the mother in your family.
- Display a statue or picture of Mary somewhere in your home.
- Read to your child *Mama, Do You Love Me?* by Barbara M. Joosse. Ask your child to describe some of the ways that a mother shows love for her children. Ask God to bless your mother and all those who love and care for others.

For more family resources, refer to the Family Activity Booklet and visit **www.loyolapress.com/preschool.**

Mother's Day Award

To a great mom
with thanks and love

Name ______________________

Circle what your father does for you.

Family Time

Special Lesson 10: Father's Day

In this lesson the children talked about ways in which fathers show love. They were encouraged in return to show love for their fathers by words and actions. They learned that God is our Father in heaven.

Your Child

Families grow closer by spending time together. Take the opportunity to share daily activities as well as special time together. Speak to your child about God as a loving Father who cares for us and loves us.

Reflect

Jesus said, "Your heavenly Father knows everything you need."
(adapted from Matthew 6:32)

Pray

Father, help us trust you always.

Do

- Let your child share in some of the tasks of the father in your family: working in the yard, cleaning the garage, washing windows, cooking.
- Visit, call, or write the grandfathers in your family.
- Have a special meal in honor of the father in your family.
- Read to your child *Daddy Makes the Best Spaghetti* by Anna Grossnickle Hines. Ask your child to describe some of the ways that a father shows love for his children. Ask God to bless your father and all those who love and care for others.

For more family resources, refer to the Family Activity Booklet and visit **www.loyolapress.com/preschool.**

You're #1

Happy Father's Day

Thank you,

Love,

____

Name ____________________________

Decorate the cake. Add flames to the candles

Family Time

Special Lesson 11: Birthdays

In this lesson the children celebrated their birthdays. They recalled that their life is a gift from God. Ask your child to show you the book about life he or she made. Have your child tell you about it.

Your Child

A birthday is an occasion to enhance your child's self-concept. Birthdays celebrate the person. Make your child's birthday special. Include a special prayer thanking God for the gift of your child to your family.

Reflect

I praise you, God, for the wonder of myself. (adapted from Psalm 139:14)

Pray

God, we praise you for the gift of life.

Do

- Look at pictures with your child that show how much he or she has grown.
- Have a birthday party and invite your child's friends.
- Serve your child's favorite food on his or her birthday.
- Show your child his or her birth certificate, bronzed shoes, hair from his or her first haircut, or other mementos of the beginning of life.
- Occasionally celebrate half-birthdays of family members.
- Hang a banner or flag inside or outside your home in honor of your child's birthday.
- Read to your child *On the Day You Were Born* by Debra Frasier. Share together some favorite memories of birthdays and other specials celebrations. Together give thanks to God for the day of your child's birth.

For more family resources, refer to the Family Activity Booklet and visit **www.loyolapress.com/preschool.**

I Thank God I'm Alive!

I can see sunsets and skyscrapers,
daisies and stars,
and people who love me.

Name ________________________________

1

I can hear music, wind in the trees,
raindrops on the roof,
and my mother calling me.

2

I can feel a kitten's fur,
the warm sun,
and a hug.

3

I can run down the street,
into the lake,
or to Grandma's house.

4

I can eat turkey, pizza, peas,
chocolate chip cookies,
strawberries,
and popcorn.

I'm alive and I'm five.
Life is great. Let's celebrate.

I can shout for joy,
whisper a secret,
and sing a song.

I can play hide-and-seek,
watch movies, feed ducks,
and snuggle under blankets on a cold night.

Name ______________________________

Finish coloring the picture.

Family Time

Special Lesson 12:
Last Class/Summer

In this lesson the children talked about the coming summer activities. They also recalled what they have learned in preschool. Ask your child to show you the certificate he or she received. Congratulate your child and display the certificate.

Your Child

During the summer, bring out some of the cards and crafts from this preschool program and review with your child what he or she learned. Do several of the finger plays and songs from the Family Activity Booklet.

Reflect

I will give thanks to you, O Lord. I will sing your praise before the world. For your kindness is as high as the sky.
(adapted from Psalm 57:10–11)

Pray

God, may we praise you with joy forever.

Do

- Continue to pray spontaneously with your child during the summer as you enjoy beautiful times together.
- Plan family activities, such as picnics, games, or attending local festivals and fairs.
- Keep a family scrapbook of the summer's activities.
- Have your family portrait taken.
- Read to your child *Summer* by Alice Low. Talk about some of the fun things you will do this summer. Pray for God's blessing on your family and on your summertime activities.

For more family resources, refer to the Family Activity Booklet and visit **www.loyolapress.com/preschool.**

This is to certify that

____

has completed the *God Made the World* preschool program.

______________________________ ______________

Catechist's Signature Date

Special Lesson 11: Birthdays

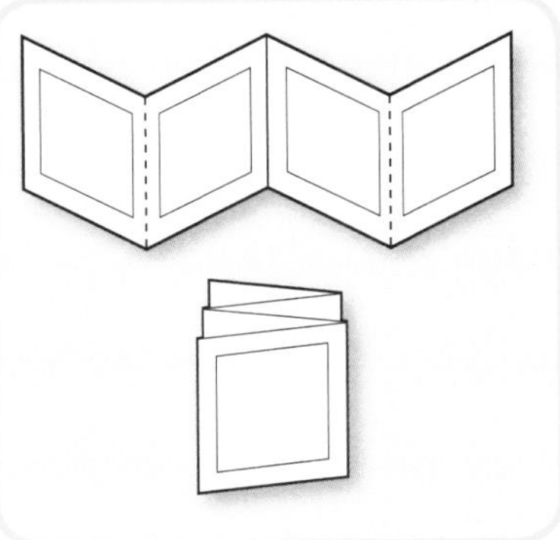

Song

To the tune of "Happy Birthday":
God, we thank you for life.
God, we thank you for life.
Our life is your good gift.
God, we thank you for life.

Craft

Accordion Birthday Book (page 153)

Cut apart the strips on the solid black line. Fold the strips on the dotted lines so that the lines on the front of the card are on the peaks. Place pages 2 and 3 next to each other and tape them together. Fold together pages 2 and 3 so that they are face-to-face. Fold up the book.

Special Lesson 12: Last Class/Summer

Finger Play

I will give thanks to you, O Lord.
I will sing your praise before the world.
For your kindness is as high as the sky. [Stretch arms toward the sky.]

Family Time

LIVING AND EXPERIENCING FAITH AT HOME is key to your child's faith formation. After each chapter, your child will bring home "Family Time," a feature that provides essential tools to help you live your faith as a family. For more ideas, visit

www.loyolapress.com/preschool

LOYOLA PRESS.
A JESUIT MINISTRY

16

Family Activity Booklet

This booklet will help you enrich lessons from your child's preschool religion class. The following songs, finger plays, and poems are for your family to enjoy at home. If a craft is to be completed at home, help your child follow the directions.

Chapter 1: God Made Me

Song

To the tune of "Twinkle, Twinkle, Little Star":

Twinkle, twinkle, little star, [Open and close fists raised high.]
God has made us what we are.
Though a million stars I see, [Sweep arms from left to right.]
You are special just like me. [Point thumb at self.]
Twinkle, twinkle, little star, [Open and close fists raised high.]
God has made us what we are.

Mary Kathleen Glavich, S.N.D.

Finger Play

I Have Two Eyes

I have two eyes that wink and blink, [Wink.]
I have a mind to make me think, [Point to head.]
I have two hands that clap for fun, [Clap.]
I have two feet that jump and run, [Jump and run in place.]
I have two ears to hear a song, [Cup ears with hands.]
Two lips to praise God all day long, [Point to lips.]
I have a body strong and good, [Put hands out at sides.]
To use for Jesus as I should.

Chapter 2: God Made My Family

Craft

Gift for the Family (page 9)

Write your name at the bottom. Make a picture or design using a sponge held with a clip clothespin and dipped in tempera paint. Alternatively, glue on pieces of fabric or torn tissue paper.

Special Lesson 8: Valentine's Day

Song

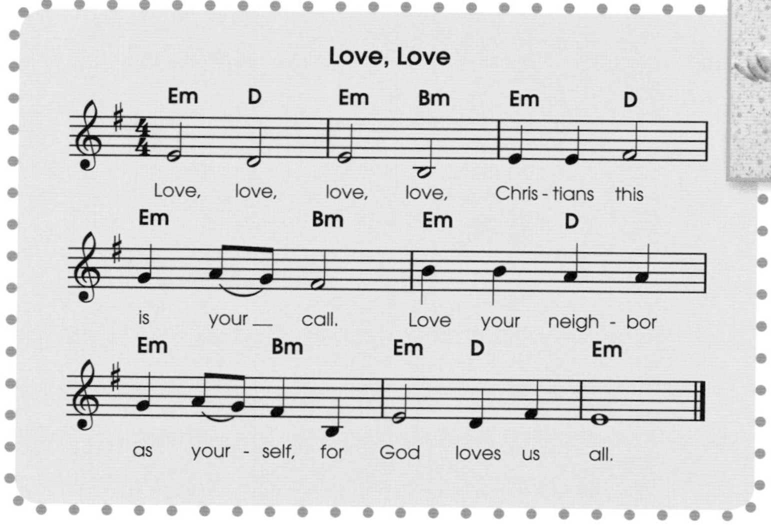

Craft

Valentine (page 141)

Cut out the two hearts. Write your name on the line. Punch holes in the small hearts around the white heart. Go into the first hole under the flower with red yarn or ribbon, leaving a tail of about five inches. Sew around the heart. Tie the ends of the yarn or ribbon to make a bow. Glue the small red heart in the middle of the white heart. Give the valentine to someone you like.

Special Lesson 9: Mother's Day

Craft

Mother's Day Scroll (page 145)

Write your name on the line. Color or paint the flowers. Roll up the scroll. Tie yarn or ribbon around the scroll to hold it together. Give it to your mother on Mother's Day.

Special Lesson 10: Father's Day

Craft

Father's Day Card (page 149)

Draw a picture in the frame of something your father does for you. Write your name. Fold the card to stand up. Give the card to your father on Father's Day.

Special Lesson 4: Lent

Craft

Footprints (page 127)

Color a part of the footprints each day you say a prayer or do a good deed during Lent.

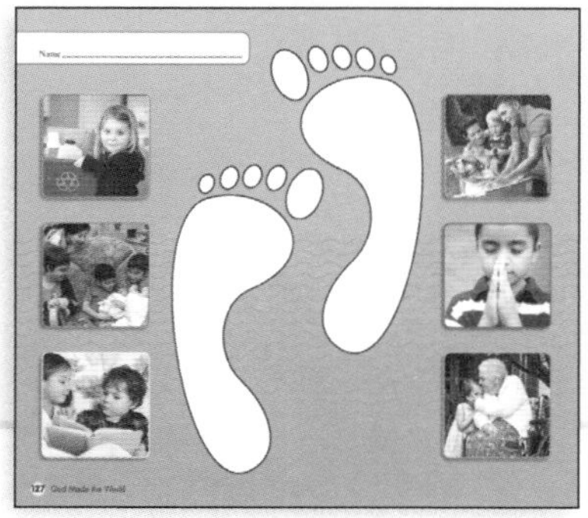

Special Lesson 5: Easter

Craft

Reversible Easter Card (page 131)

Color the sun yellow. Fold the sides of the card forward to cover the sun. Open the card to show darkness giving way to the sun. Fold the sides the other way so that the card shows an egg and, when the sides are opened, a chick.

Special Lesson 6: Pentecost

Poem

God Is There

When I run in the sun,
God is there, God is there.
When I fall playing ball,
God cares, God cares.
When I'm sad or I'm glad,
God knows, God knows.
When I mind or I'm kind,
God sees, God sees.
God is with me day and night,
Help me to do what's right.
I love you, God!

Mary Kathleen Glavich, S.N.D.

Special Lesson 7: Thanksgiving

Poem

Turkey Time

Thanksgiving Day will soon be here;
It comes around but once a year.
If I could only have my way,
We'd have Thanksgiving every day!

Craft

Stand-Up Turkey (page 137)

Trace your hand in the center section. Your thumb becomes the turkey's head and neck; your four fingers become tail feathers. (You might purchase real feathers at a craft store.) Add legs. Color or paint the turkey. Fold back the two sides on the dotted lines.

Chapter 3: God Made My Friends

Song

To the tune of "Did You Ever See a Lassie?":
The more we are together, together, together,
The more we are together, the happier we'll be.
For your friends are my friends,
And my friends are your friends.
The more we are together, the happier we'll be.

Craft

Flower (page 13)

Write your name under the words "I love you" on the back of the flower. Color the flower (or staple a few circles of colored tissue paper to the center and pull them up around the staple). Cut off the stem and then cut the line between the flower and grass. Finish cutting out the flower. Glue the grass and flower to the stem.

Chapter 4: God Made My Helpers

Craft

Card for a Helper (page 17)

Fold the card in half. Inside the card, draw a picture of the person who helps you. Write your name inside the card.

Chapter 5: God Made My Church Family

Song

To the tune of "Row, Row, Row Your Boat":

Women, men, girls, and boys, [Point to several people.]
Mary, saints, and me— [Point up and then to self.]
All are members of God's Church. [Extend arms wide.]
We're God's family. [Clap twice at the end.]

Mary Kathleen Glavich, S.N.D.

Craft

Photo Frame of God's Family (page 21)

Cut out and glue the pictures of Mary and the other Church members in the matching spaces. Draw yourself in the last space. Keep the extra picture of Jesus as a reminder to love as Jesus loves.

Chapter 6: God Made Churches

Finger Play

Here is the church. [Interlace fingers, fold hands, knuckles on top, thumbs together pointing up.]
Here is the steeple. [Point index fingers up, fingertips touching.]
Open the doors, [Turn hands over with fingers still interlaced.]
And see all the people. [Wiggle fingers.]

Craft

Church (page 25)

Cut off the strip of pictures and cut out the altar and the cross. Glue the cross in place on the back of the page. Glue the altar in front of the priest. Fold the church in thirds so that it stands. Cut the doors on the black lines and fold them on the dotted lines so that they open.

Chapter 7: God Made the Bible

Craft

Letter from God (page 29)

Write your name on the front and back of the letter. Cut off the side strip and fold and tape the letter closed.

Special Lesson 2: Advent

Finger Play

Hush! The world is waiting— [Raise finger to lips.]
Waiting for Baby Jesus. [Rock arms.]
Mary and Joseph are waiting— [Extend one arm, then the other.]
Waiting for Mary's Son. [Rock arms.]
Shepherds and kings are waiting— [Extend one arm, then the other.]
Waiting for the newborn king. [Rock arms.]
I am waiting— [Point to self.]
Waiting for my Savior. [Extend arms up.]

Mary Kathleen Glavich, S.N.D.

Craft

Manger (page 119)

Cut in on the four black lines. Fold down the edge with the star to meet the other star. Fold down the edge with the flower to meet the other flower. Fold the four sides so that they stand. Overlap the ends and tape them together. Use yellow yarn or strips of paper for straw.

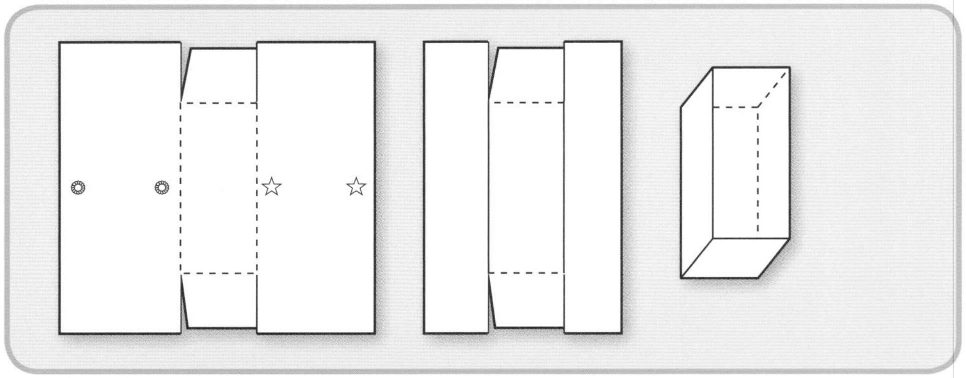

Special Lesson 3: Christmas

Craft

Christmas Tree (page 123)

Put round stickers or star stickers on the tree, being careful not to put them on the lines. If you do not have stickers, paint or color decorations. You might add glitter and sequins. Write your name on the line. Cut out the tree and the square with the star. Cut a slit in the tree's top on the heavy black line. Fold the tree on the dotted lines and tape or staple it together. Insert the star into the slit at the top.

4

13

Chapter 25: God Made Laughter

Song

Craft

Party Hat (page 111)

Cut out the hat and bend and staple it to make a cone. Staple or tape two pieces of yarn to the hat—one at each square—for ties. If you wish, staple or tape a pom-pom to the top of the hat.

Special Lesson 1: Halloween/Feast of All Saints

Craft

Crown (page 115)

Write your name on the line. Color the jewels on the crown. If you wish, add glitter or sequins. Cut out the crown and the strip of paper. Staple the strip to one end of the crown. Put on the crown and staple the other end of the strip to it so that the crown fits.

Chapter 8: God Made Music

Song

Craft

Banner (page 35)

Cut apart the banner from the green strip of paper. Cut the banner along the diagonal lines and decorate it. Starting with one corner, roll the green strip of paper around a pencil to make a stick. Tape it together and remove the pencil. Tape or staple the banner to the "stick."

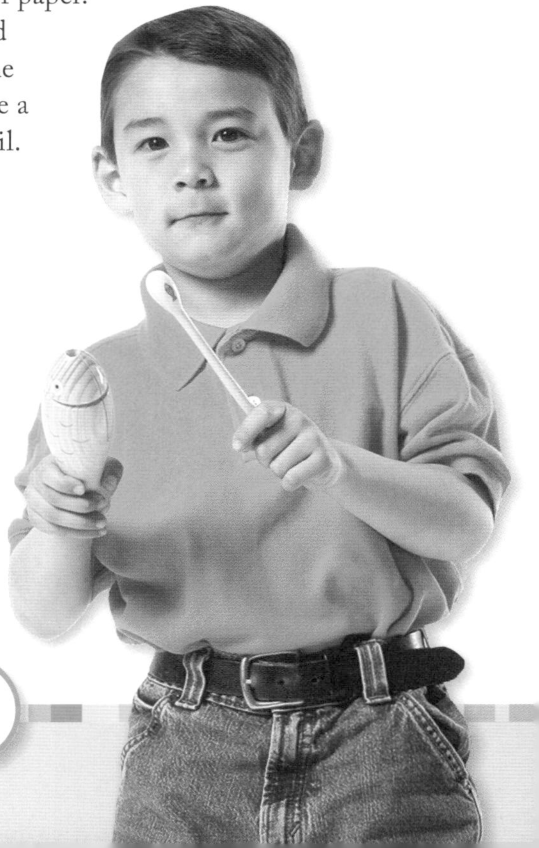

Chapter 9: God Made Water

Song

To the tune of "Here We Go 'Round the Mulberry Bush":

This is the way we wash our clothes,
wash our clothes, wash our clothes.
This is the way we wash our clothes,
with the gift of water.

2. This is the way we water the yard . . .
3. This is the way we brush our teeth . . .
4. This is the way we quench our thirst . . .
5. This is the way we cook our food . . .
6. This is the way we swim in the pool . . .

Craft

Water Scene (page 39)

Dip pieces of blue yarn in a mixture of water and white glue. Squeeze each piece through your fingers to get rid of the excess glue. Arrange the yarn on the paper to look like curvy waves. Add glitter to represent light on the water.

Chapter 10: God Made Food

Craft

Place Mat (page 43)

Decorate the place mat by painting it or make designs on the mat, using the end of a pencil eraser or glue stick tube dipped in paint. Cut fringe around the sides or make the sides wavy or jagged.

Chapter 11: God Made Land

Song

He's Got the Whole World

1. He's got the whole world in his hands. [four times]
2. He's got the towering mountains in his hands.
3. He's got the peaceful valleys in his hands.
4. He's got the busy cities in his hands.
5. He's got the lovely farmlands in his hands.
6. He's got the hot, dry deserts in his hands.

Craft

Earth Mobile (page 49)

If you wish, cut out the picture of the earth. Draw or glue pictures of land features (forests, fields, mountains) in the four sections on the back. Punch a hole in the top of the mobile. String yarn or ribbon through the hole to form a loop. Hang up your mobile where everyone can see it and remember to care for God's gift of the earth.

Chapter 22: God Made Big Things

Finger Play

The elephant goes like this and that	[Hold one hand over the other and sway arms from side to side.]
He's oh, so big, and he's oh, so fat.	[Curve arms outward.]
He has no fingers, and he has no toes.	[Hold hand in front with fingers closed.]
But goodness gracious, what a nose!	[Extend arms up with fingers intertwined.]

Craft

Thank-You Card for God (page 99)

Decorate or draw pictures on the page with things that God made. Write your name on it. (Parents may write "Thank you, God" on the card.)

Chapter 23: God Made Little Things

Craft

Pet Pocket (page 103)

Cut apart the four pet cards and fold them so that they stand. Cut out the pocket and fold it on the dotted line. Staple or glue the sides of the pocket together. Put the pets inside. Add a four-inch piece of yarn as a pet worm.

Chapter 24: God Made Countries

Craft

A Country's Flag (page 107)

Choose a flag and draw it in the empty space above the flags. Cut off the section with the many flags. Roll the long piece of paper up to your flag and tape or staple it to form a stick. If you prefer, draw the flag on the longer piece of paper and tape it to a straw or a craft stick. Tell your child which country's flag he or she has chosen.

Chapter 20: God Made Fish

Finger Play

I am a fish in the great blue sea.
God made me as happy as can be.
I swim all day and sleep all night.
To be God's fish is my delight.

[Put hands together with thumbs crossed and "swim."]

Mary Kathleen Glavich, S.N.D.

Craft

Fish Picture (page 89)

Decorate the large fish with crayons or markers. Place the page in a box with a marble that has been dipped in white tempera paint. Tilt the box from side to side so that the marble leaves tracks that make a net.

Chapter 21: God Made Butterflies

Song

To the tune of "Happy Birthday":
God our Father, thank you
For all that you do.
You're full of surprises.
How much we love you!

Mary Kathleen Glavich, S.N.D.

Poem

Little Arabella Miller

Little Arabella Miller
Found a woolly caterpillar.
First it crawled upon her mother,
Then upon her baby brother.
All said, "Arabella Miller,
Take away that caterpillar!"

Craft

3-D Butterfly Picture (page 93)

Cut off the side strip and cut out the two butterflies. Fold the butterflies on the dotted lines. Color the flower. Put glue on the white part of the wings of the two butterflies and place the butterflies on the picture.

Chapter 12: God Made Air

Finger Play

The wind tells me, [Sway.]
The birds tell me, [Flap arms.]
The Bible tells me too, [Open hands like a book.]
How much our Father loves us all, [Stretch out arms.]
And now I'm telling you! [Point to self and then point out.]

Craft

Kite (page 53)

Decorate the yellow part with designs or pictures. Cut off the multicolored strip and the white triangle. Fold the two blue sides to meet in the back and tape them together. Staple or tape the multicolored strip to the bottom to make the kite's tail. Tape yarn to the tail. Run with the kite to make it fly.

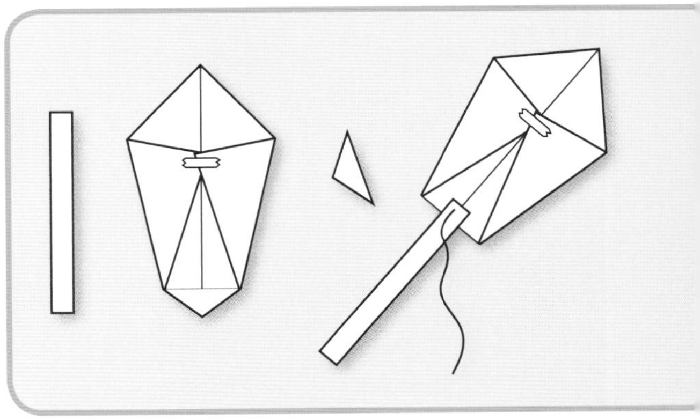

Chapter 13: God Made Light

Song

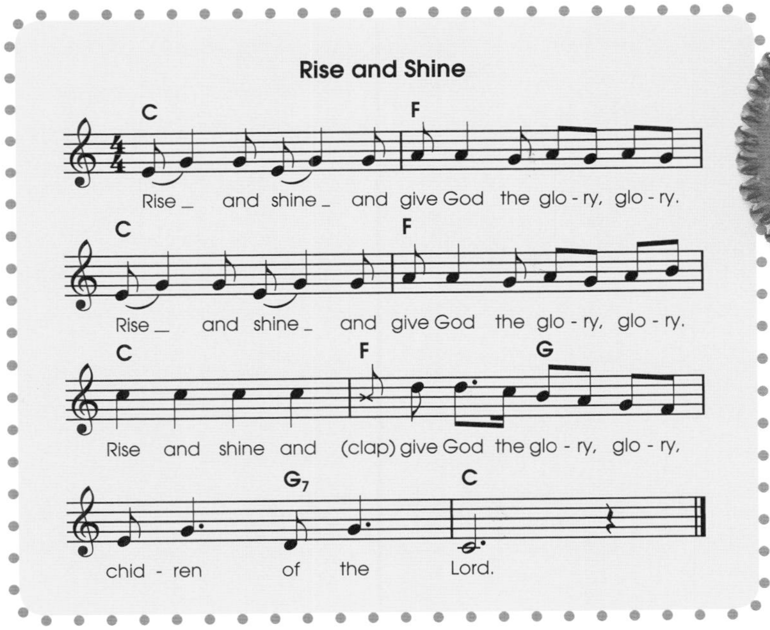

Craft

Candle (page 57)

Color the flowers. Write your name on the line above the flowers. Cut off the strip with the flame on it. Roll the large piece of the page and tape it together. Glue or tape the flame to the top of the candle.

Chapter 14: God Made Color

Craft

Book of Colors (page 61)

Fold the page in half on the dotted line. On each page, color the picture the same color as the balloon beside or above it. Draw more things that are the color of the balloon. Draw things that belong to you.

Chapter 15: God Made Weather

Craft

Weather Wheel (page 65)

Cut slits in the wheel along the lines. Color the sun yellow. Color the raindrops blue. Cut the strip from the page. Fold the page on the dotted line so that it stands. Put the ends of the strip through the slits in the wheel. (The strip should slide back and forth to show the pictures.) Change the wheel to match the day's weather.

Chapter 16: God Made Flowers

Finger Play

This is my garden.	[Extend hand, palm up.]
I'll rake it with care.	[Make pulling motion with hands.]
And plant some flower seeds Right in there.	[Make planting motions with thumb and index finger.]
The sun will shine,	[Make circle with arms above head.]
The rain will fall.	[Flutter fingers downward.]
And my garden will blossom And grow straight and tall.	[Cup hands; raise them slowly.]

Craft

Basket of Flowers (page 69)

Color the flowers. Cut off the strip at the side, which is the handle. Staple one end of the strip to the corner of the large square where there is a blue dot. Staple the other end to the opposite corner so that the ends of the square are pulled up to form a basket. Give the basket to someone you love.

8

Chapter 17: God Made Trees

Craft

Tree (page 73)

Add leaves to the tree in one of these ways: 1) draw them with crayons or markers; 2) dip sponges in tempera paint and press them to the branches; 3) glue on pieces of green or red, yellow, and orange tissue paper, torn construction paper, or fabric; 4) glue on real leaves.

Chapter 18: God Made Animals

Finger Play

There was a little turtle. He lived in a box.
He swam in a puddle. He climbed on the rocks.
He snapped at a mosquito. He snapped at a flea.
He snapped at a minnow, and he snapped at me.
He caught the mosquito. He caught the flea.
He caught the minnow, but he didn't catch me.

[Add snapping gestures with with thumb and fingers of one hand when the turtle snaps.]

Craft

Animal Box (page 81)

Cut out the four yellow squares. Fold up the sides of the box so that the green is inside. Tape the ends together. Fold the yellow squares along the diagonal and stand the animals in the box.

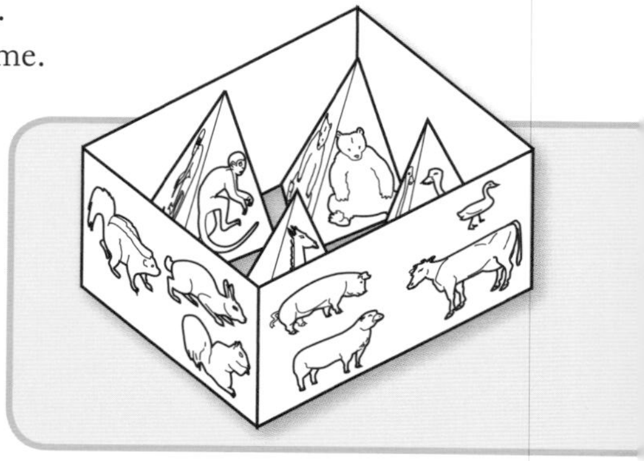

Chapter 19: God Made Birds

Finger Play

Thank you for the world so sweet,	[Put out right hand.]
Thank you for the food we eat,	[Put out left hand.]
Thank you for the birds that sing,	[Raise hands.]
Thank you, God, for everything.	[Extend hands to side.]

Craft

Bird Mobile (page 85)

Cut apart the three sections. Tape an end of a piece of yarn to each bird. Tape the other ends of the yarn to the strip. Punch a hole in the top of the strip. Thread yarn through the hole and tie it to make a loop for hanging the mobile.

9